Through the Eyes of SoulCollage®

The SoulCollage® card you see on the cover of this book is calling "Seeing True." Here is what this card said to me in my journal:

I Am the One Who looks at the world with wonder and joy. I Am the One Who yearns for new visions. I Am the One Who seeks to see what's out there. I Am the One Who takes in the lessons from what I see. I Am the One Who looks through the window of my life and sees the extraordinary. I am happiest when I am riding the pink sailboat seas of my imagination. I Am the One Who brings the mystery of life closer by using SoulCollage®.

My gift to you is vision, clear sight, insight, and the ability to paint your inner skies with rainbows whenever you choose.

My message for you today is this: keep looking, keep seeing true. Keep visioning with your inner and outer eye. Absorb whatever you see and transform it into wisdom through the process of SoulCollage®.

TODAY I WANT You TO KNOW; u

Through the Eyes of SoulCollage®

Reflections on Life Via the SoulCollage® Lens

Anne Marie Bennett

87 Thought-Provoking Essays That Explore
Life Lessons
Community Suit
Animal Companions Suit
Spirituality
Using Your SoulCollage® Cards

ISBN: 1516963849
ISBN 13: 9781516963843
Library of Congress Control Number: 2015913722
CreateSpace Independent Publishing Platform
North Charleston, South Carolina

Images on cover collage purchased on Dreamstime.com
©Lightkeeper, ©13claudio13, ©Haywiremedia, ©Valery121283, ©Elecstasy

This book is lovingly dedicated to:

Seena, who gave us all the gift of SoulCollage®

Noelle, who helped me to open the gift

Kylea, who showed me how to use the gift

Karen, who companioned me
during my early years of facilitating

and

Elaine, Lis, Pat, Susan and Linda,
who joined me at my dining room table
for many a joyful Sunday afternoon
as we continued to explore
the gift of SoulCollage®
together.

Permission is granted by Hanford Mead Publishers Inc. for use of quotations from *SoulCollage® Evolving* (2010) by Seena B. Frost.

With thanks to Kylea Taylor, Dot Everhart and Elizabeth Cunningham for allowing me to quote them as well!

Alan Cohen quotation used by permission. www.AlanCohen.com

Dip into this collection of Anne Marie's life stories, and you will discover many ideas for your own personal SoulCollage® deck. She describes how very different Neters came to live in her deck, and you will be surprised and charmed. You might just be nudged to search for images to create new cards for your own deck! This book will help you discover the wisdom hidden in your own imagination.

~ Seena B. Frost, Founder of SoulCollage® and author of *SoulCollage® Evolving*

AND

This is a wonderful book! It is really an important contribution to the SoulCollage® literature.

~ Kylea Taylor, President of SoulCollage Inc. and author of *The Ethics of Caring*

Table of Contents

Introduction

THIS BOOK IS the culmination of the last 10 deeply-satisfying years of my own SoulCollage® journey. As soon as I discovered the gift that is SoulCollage®, I sought out as many ways as I could to offer it to the world. One of these ways turned out to be my website, KaleidoSoul.com, which has reached thousands of people worldwide.

About a year after beginning KaleidoSoul, I began offering a Kindred Spirits yearly membership, which gives curious and avid SoulCollagers access to many audio recordings as well as other juicy, delightful online SoulCollage® benefits. One of these benefits is a weekly SoulCollage®-focused newsletter called *Soul Treasures*. Every other week I write an essay for our members' newsletter that pertains, in some way, to SoulCollage®.

As I continued my monthly practice of writing these essays, I discovered that I was looking at the world through SoulCollage® eyes. It seemed that no matter where I was, and no matter what happened to me, when I looked at it through the lens of SoulCollage®, I discovered something new about myself; I was able to dive a little deeper into my own soul.

Since 2015 is KaleidoSoul's 10th anniversary, I thought it would be good to combine my columns into one book. Of course, there are too many for one book, which is why you are only holding Volume 1 in your hands right now! It has been a rewarding experience for me to reread what I've written over the years and to group them into categories for your reading pleasure.

Some of these essays share life lessons I have learned over the years; some focus in on our animal companions; some point towards the importance of community; some are centered on the mystery of the spiritual, and some include ways to actively use your SoulCollage® cards. Volume 2 will contain other topics to round out the journey.

My wish in offering you this book is that you will become more and more aware of the large and small blessings that SoulCollage® offers you moment to moment, day by day, year after year. May you pick up this book when you need a lift, a hug of encouragement, a smile, an understanding, or a simple reminder that you are connected to the wider SoulCollage® community.

I wish you much peace and joy. May your own SoulCollage® journey be abundant and rich. May you continue to look at what is going on in your life with your own SoulCollage® eyes. May you discover new layers and deeper meanings for your life.

Anne Marie Bennett
Beverly, MA
September, 2015

Vocabulary

HERE ARE SOME of the words I use throughout the book, and my own short definitions of them as informed by Seena Frost in her book *SoulCollage® Evolving*:

Archetypes- These are themes or motifs that play out over our individual lives.

Committee Suit- These are cards that we make to represent our inner voices or personality parts. We'll go into more detail on the Committee in Volume 2.

Community Suit- These are cards that we make to represent family, friends, teachers, pets and those sentient beings whose lives have touched our own.

Companions- These are cards we make to honor the animal guides who live in each of our body's chakras.

Council Suit- These are cards that we make to represent archetypal energies that have touched our lives. We'll go into more detail on the Council in Volume 2.

Deck- This is a set of SoulCollage® cards that represent various parts of one's life journey. It includes the above suits as well as cards that symbolize The One.

Neter- We refer to each card, or energy, in our decks as a Neter, which is an ancient Egyptian word that meant "The One" as well as "The Many."

Suit- A SoulCollage® deck often consists of four suits or categories that represent a different part of our life. The four suits as introduced by Seena Frost are: Committee, Community, Companions, and Council.

The One- You can choose to call "The One" from which all else springs by any name that appeals to you. Some people call it Source; others call it The Divine, God, or Allah.

The Many- This is the term we use for all the parts and pieces of our lives, as represented by the four suits.

How to Use This Book

Time for Reflection

At the end of each essay, I've offered some suggestions for how you can relate my story to your own life and your own work with SoulCollage®. There are card making ideas, journaling ideas, and lots of other creative ideas too! Feel free to use these or adapt them for your own personal use.

SoulCollage® Examples

In some of my stories, I describe one of my own SoulCollage® cards. At the end of each of these particular essays, you will find a link to a page on my website where you can take a peek at this card. Please be aware that each of these pages is password protected so be sure to note the password given before opening the web page.

SoulCollage® does not advocate copying or infringing on the copyrighted work of others in any way. SoulCollage® cards are made for personal use. Part of personal use is sharing. When I share my personal stories, I also want to share my cards with you.

SoulCollage® Resources

Once in a while, I have added a resource for your reference. I hope you find these recommended books and websites helpful.

If You Are New to SoulCollage®

1. Start at the beginning with the very first essay. Read one every couple of days, and at the same time, read Seena's book *SoulCollage® Evolving*, or some of the content pages at KaleidoSoul.com.

2. Skim through the *Table of Contents* and *Vocabulary* listing at the beginning of this book. Listen inside yourself for what most intrigues you and start with *that* section first. You might want to read a few essays within that topic and let your reading inspire you to make some cards.

3. After you've made some cards based on the suggestions in the Time for Reflection offered after each essay, try out some of the ideas in the last section: *Using Your SoulCollage® Cards.*

If You Are an Experienced SoulCollager

1. Start at the beginning. Read one essay per week and spend some quality time with the "Time for Reflection" section at the end.

2. Choose the section that you're most curious about and start there instead of at the beginning.

3. Open the book at random and read whatever essay you land on. Take it to heart. Do the "Time for Reflection" exercises at the end, or make up your own!

Suggestions for Facilitators

I DIDN'T WRITE these essays with SoulCollage® Facilitators in mind, but I've had many Facilitators tell me that they've been inspired to create workshops based on what they've read. With that in mind, here are some ways to use this book if you are a SoulCollage® Facilitator.

1. Choose a topic that you're not completely comfortable explaining to others. Start with that section. Read the essays and do the "Time for Reflection" exercises for yourself until you feel more comfortable with this topic.

2. Start at the beginning and read each essay until you come to one that stirs you up inside. You'll notice your creative juices starting to flow! Create a workshop theme that revolves around the topic of this essay. Use the "Time for Reflection" activities or journaling questions to share with your workshop participants. Create your own SoulCollage® card or cards on this topic to share as well.

3. Give each person in your monthly group a copy of this book. Invite each person to share their favorite essay at your next gathering, as well as a SoulCollage® card they were inspired to create as a result of it.

4. Read aloud one of the essays to your workshop participants. Invite them to discuss the topic in dyads, small groups, or the large group. Allow time for card making afterwards.

Life Lessons

Overview

At the time of publication, I am 59 years old, which means that I've lived long enough to have been faced with major opportunities for some really indispensable lessons in living. Having the process of SoulCollage® in order to frame these lessons has been invaluable to me on my own life's journey, and I have learned even more about myself in the retelling of these lessons here.

Where have I learned these lessons? During dog walks, on an airplane, while watching a television show, in my doctor's office, and at the library. Sitting in the audience of a Broadway musical, and behind the scenes at community theatre auditions. From the wilds of Alaska to an inner city traffic court setting and everywhere in between. Because I remain open to these lessons, and because I welcome them with a curious heart, I seem to find them everywhere!

Who helped me to learn these lessons? My dad, a former doctor, our oldest granddaughter, beloved teachers at Kripalu, our dog Suzy, my big brothers, a favorite book character, and some little girls in pink tutus at the YMCA (to name a few).

The Life Lessons I've included in this volume touch on joy and sadness, love and laughter, loss, courage, and more. When translated through the lens of SoulCollage®, these emotional journeys become less intimidating and more inspiring. I hope that each Lesson I've learned will make some small difference in your own life, and that you will be inspired to be open to and aware of all the life lessons that cross your path as well.

CHAPTER 1

Doing the Next Thing

IN MY THIRTIES, I liked to take personal retreats at a lovely retreat center out in the countryside of northern Massachusetts. Each retreater had her own little "hermitage" and there was a quarter of a mile walk up to the main house where meals were served and Morning/Evening Prayer services were held by the Brothers who ran the center.

I will never forget the first time I went there. It was mid-autumn; the air was crisp and cold, scented with falling leaves. The walk from Evening Prayer back to my cottage that night was *very* dark. Luckily, the Brothers had given each of us a flashlight to light our way back to our cottages. I had lingered a while in the library after the Evening Prayer service, so I was walking alone. I knew the general direction of my hermitage, but I couldn't actually *see* it. I could only see as far ahead as the glow from my flashlight, so that is how I made the whole journey from the retreat center's main building to my hermitage, one little glow at a time.

At first I was afraid because I really couldn't see where I was going, but after several steps I realized that *I didn't need to see the whole pathway*. I just needed to follow the beam of the flashlight, and that was just enough to take me all the way home.

Looking back, I see now that this is a brilliant metaphor for life. I may not be able to see my final destination on any given journey (career, health, relationships), but *as long as I follow the light I am given in this moment*, I can trust that I will stay on the path, arriving at the right time and place.

The same is true of our SoulCollage® journeys. When I first started making cards, I was quite guilty of needing to "know" where I was headed, where the card was headed, and what it all meant. After about 20 cards, I got the hang of just *doing the next thing, taking the next step*, even though I didn't know why, even though I didn't know where the card was taking me.

This is true of how we actually make the cards - choosing images, letting images choose us, laying out a card, and gluing down the individual pieces. It's also true of the journaling and readings that we do with our cards.

Just trust yourself. Simply do the next thing, and you will always be shown the next step.

Time for Reflection

The next time you make a SoulCollage® card, stop yourself before you begin. Shake out your hands, your mind and your body. Let go of any preconceived notions of what this card might be about. Let go of control. And just do the next thing. Choose the next image and glue it down without even worrying about what you'll do next. Stay in the moment and trust the process. Leave the past and the future out of it completely and just *be with what is* as you create the card. To do this, you need to stay out of your rational left brain, and move more fully into your right-brained, intuitive, trusting, flowing self.

CHAPTER 2

Lessons in Learning

I WALKED BY the young peoples' gym at the local YMCA the other day and saw a group of children stepping for the first time onto a low balance beam. It was easy to see each of them as a brilliant metaphor for how we learn something new in many different ways.

A little girl in pink tights and sparkly top practically danced her way across the wooden beam as if she were born doing it. A slim boy with tousled curly hair needed help the entire time, and he gladly let the teacher guide him across, holding his arms out in T-position. Another child pushed the teacher away when offered help, then stumbled and fell onto the bright blue vinyl mat, crying.

I smiled as I walked away from the gym that day. It depends on what I'm learning, but I can definitely identify with each one of those children.

When I first found SoulCollage®, I felt as though I'd been born doing it. It felt easy, like dancing to my favorite song on the radio. Taking Physics in my first year of college was way out of my league, but I liked the professor and stayed after class for many weeks as I learned the ins and outs of this challenging topic. Languages usually come easy to me but when I started Spanish class for my foreign language requirement in college, I felt like I was a stranger in a strange land. I struggled and resisted and whined (and yes, I failed at first) until a friend took pity on me and gave me some private lessons.

I've learned over the years to be gentle with myself whenever I'm starting something new. Whether it's learning a new collage technique, creating a website, or figuring out a new knitting pattern, I have found that my learning is smoother and less fraught with tension if I simply let go of my preconceived notions of how it all "should" be happening, and if I stop beating myself up for not learning quickly enough.

Time for Reflection

Take a look at your own life this week. Are you in the process of learning something new, either at work or in your personal life?

Pay attention to the inner Committee voices that come up when you are learning this new thing. What thoughts are going through your mind as you think of succeeding or failing?

Do you have SoulCollage® cards for any of these parts? Give one of them a voice whether you have a card for it or not. Listen to its story. Why is it intent on stopping you? How is it helping you?

Can you also hear a different voice inside, a voice that is cheering you on in your quest for new learning? Make a SoulCollage® card to honor this cheerleader part of you also.

CHAPTER 3

Asking the Important Questions

THERE IS SO much that I want to do with my time. So many choices! Shall I create SoulCollage® cards, write short stories, actively market my second book, journal with my SoulCollage® cards, play guitar, get together with friends, do readings with my cards, play around with altered books, watercolor, spend time journaling and art journaling, read that stack of books on my nightstand...? Well, you get the idea! Sometimes it feels like a struggle, just listening to all of these yearnings inside of me.

When the many different voices of my passions threaten to over-whelm me, I try to remember that struggling to choose just one of them isn't necessarily an option. I have struggled all my life with trying to rein in my creativity, and I just don't want to do that anymore!

When this sense of overwhelm threatens to eradicate my serenity, the key for me is to take a deep breath and listen within. I ask myself these questions: What does my soul *really* want right now? What do I need in this moment? Which part of me is asking for attention?

The answer might be a walk in the woods, a nap, or a few hours at my art table creating SoulCollage® cards. I might discover that my rebellious inner child needs some TLC, or that my inner writer needs to actually sit still and write all afternoon. Or... the answer might be: none of the above. And that's okay too.

The crucial action is to become quiet all over and to ask myself those questions. No more struggling to do it all at once; no more struggling to get "there." This is what I've found- there is no *there* to get to. There is only *here*. There is only right here, right now, this moment.

Time for Reflection

What do you really need right now, in this moment? How can you give this to yourself in some way (big or small) this week?

Get quiet and listen within. Which parts of you are clamoring for attention? Which parts of your inner world are asking for expression? Can you honor one of these parts by making a SoulCollage® card for it this week?

CHAPTER 4

Just Say No

I REMEMBER A time in my early thirties when I was having some, shall we say, "codependent issues" with my boyfriend Dan. I had worked myself into an unhealthy state of isolation (although I couldn't see that then) and felt like I was drowning in this man's problems. He was living with me; I was supporting him. I pretty much had no life of my own anymore.

I knew I needed help, so I drove three hours to spend the afternoon with my big brother John who is a social worker and family therapist specializing in addiction and codependency. After listening to me for over an hour, he did something unusual. He asked me to stand up. Then he stood in front of me and told me to say "No" to him. Not just once, but many times, over and over. He encouraged me to imagine that Dan was standing in front of me as I said "No" again and again, louder and louder each time.

At first I couldn't do it! I collapsed into giggles on the sofa. But he kept encouraging me and pretty soon I was shouting angry "NO"s that could be heard on the other side of town. It was a clear moment of awakening for me. I finally realized that I had the option to say "No" to anyone or anything that wasn't for my highest good. Up until that moment, I had no idea that this was a possibility.

After that, I actually was able to go back to my apartment and say to my boyfriend, "You need to find your own place to live." And guess what? He did! This gave me back a piece of my self that I had forgotten existed.

I urge you to find a way to say "No" to something or someone this week. Perhaps there is someone who is infringing on your personal time.

Maybe a job situation or relationship has become intolerable. There might be an inner voice that is berating or judging you. I promise that when you say NO in a big way and really mean it, you will feel a wonderful, joyful YES bubbling up in your whole being.

Time for Reflection

What do you need to say NO to in your life, in order to allow the YES to come through?

If you can relate to this, I urge you to practice saying NO out loud when you are alone in your car. Scream it, chant it, sing it, quack it like a duck if you have to, but say it out loud over and over until you are comfortable with the feel of it on your lips.

CHAPTER 5

Be Joyful

WHEN I THINK of joyful people, I am immediately reminded of two special women from my life.

Jill was a young woman I worked with several years ago. She was a tall Tigger disguised with long straw-blonde hair and bright blue eyes. Her joy was contagious; it spilled out of her and radiated from her like a stream of sweet sunshine. Her energy was buoyant and some of it always brushed off on those of us who were nearby.

The other woman was Hazel, who passed away a few years ago at the age of 91. She was my mother's best friend, and she personified joy in a very different manner. Hazel was a petite gray-haired woman who loved to sit and read, to write long entries in her journal, to pray with people. She had gifts for listening and healing. Hers was a quiet, deep joy, and it also settled on the souls of the people who came in contact with her.

Even though Jill and Hazel were very different on the outside, they had one important thing in common - a deep self-acceptance. *Each woman knew who she was and was comfortable with that.* Could there be anything more joyful than this?

Time for Reflection

Make a SoulCollage® Committee card for the joyful woman who lives inside of *you!*

Make a SoulCollage® Community card for someone whose joy has permeated your own life.

CHAPTER 6

I'm Not a Duck?

SEVERAL YEARS AGO a nearby theatre staged a production of the musical *Honk!* Based on the story of the Ugly Duckling, it was performed by adults in creative costumes which gave the impression that they were animals.

I was working in the box office there at the time, so I was lucky to be able to see *Honk!* several times during its three-week run. My favorite scene in the show was near the end, when the actor portraying the Ugly Duckling reappeared wearing starched white jeans, a pristine white ski jacket, dark sunglasses, and a brand new (also white!) baseball cap.

Ugly suddenly noticed that he wasn't wearing scruffy, torn clothes and nerdy glasses anymore, and said in total bewilderment, "I'm not a duck?" Then his amazement turned to joy as he shouted more confidently, "I'm *not* a *duck*. I'm a *swan*!" I can still hear the inflection in the character's voice as he reveled in his new-found beauteous transformation with awe and pride.

I took a lesson home with me every night from that show. I also took an affirmation-

I'm not a duck...I'm a swan.

I'm not a duck...I'm a swan.

And then I turned that affirmation into a ritual.

On my daily walks that summer, I passed a house which had two verdigris duck statues on the stone wall on either side of the driveway. When I came to them, I would touch the first duck and say to myself, "I'm not a duck." Then I would touch the second duck and say, "I'm a swan." And I would do the exact same thing on my way back home.

This little ritual is one that still brings me comfort and joy. Every time I touch those ducks and say those words, I am reminded that I really *am* a swan- with goodness, beauty, gifts, and something important to say.

Time for Reflection

Create an affirmation of your own and incorporate it into a ritual that reminds you of *your* goodness, beauty, and gifts.

Make a SoulCollage® card for your own transformation (inner or outer) from "Ugly Duckling" to "Swan."

CHAPTER 7

You Are Enough

SOMEONE ONCE ASKED the Dalai Lama what he thought we should do about the problem of self-hatred that is so prevalent in the world today. There were several interpreters present as he was speaking at a huge conference of meditation teachers.

After spending more than thirty minutes with the interpreters, he finally announced that he couldn't answer the question, because he didn't *understand* the question. It seems that there is no word or reference point in the Tibetan language/culture for the concept of self-hatred. None of the interpreters were able to convey the meaning to him, no matter how they tried to explain it.

I heard this story at a retreat a while ago and it's been keeping me company ever since. It is so hard to imagine living in a world where the concept of self-loathing is nonexistent. All I can do is try to visualize my own life without it, and then attempt to live into that image. So I've been doing exactly that.

About a year ago I was working with my therapist on the concept of feeling like I was "not enough." I made a SoulCollage® card to pay respect to the part of me who has always felt this way. I did a lot of work with this inner voice, and also with the voices who made this part feel this way.

Eventually I also made a card for the part of me who *is enough*, just as I am.

Since then I've noticed that the voices that made me feel *not enough* (a lifetime's worth of old ancestral tapes and media messages) have quieted to such a low hush that my previous self-hatred now feels like a distant memory. I still have words for it, though.

I will never be like the Dalai Lama who has no idea what self-loathing actually is. But the work I've done has dulled its intensity and stripped it of its power to get in the way of who I really am.

This is one of the main reasons why I'm so passionate about SoulCollage®. It has such tremendous power to get me in touch with what's happening inside of me, and to find the light amidst the shadow.

Time for Reflection

Take some time this week to ponder this topic. Be excruciatingly honest with yourself. Do you hate yourself, or some little part of yourself, even just a fraction of a tiny bit? Do you ever feel like you are "not enough?"

Journal with this part of you. Make a SoulCollage® card for the part of you who feels this way.

Seek out images for a card that shows how you feel when you believe that you *are* enough.

Engage in inner conversation with all of these parts, and over time, you will find their power to hurt you lessens and releases.

SoulCollage® Examples

Please visit kaleidosoul.com/inner-journeys-growth
The password for this page is grow

The topic to scroll down to is:
Enough

CHAPTER 8

Do What Makes You Twinkle

SEVERAL MONTHS AGO, my Primary Care Physician moved away, so I shopped around for a new one. Finally settling on a woman doctor (I'll call her Dr. Judy) close to home, I made an appointment for my annual physical.

As we chatted, Dr. Judy studiously took notes on a laptop computer, hardly making eye contact. I noticed this immediately; it felt like she wasn't paying attention to me. In the course of our conversation, she asked me if I exercised. I told her that I really liked to swim, although I hadn't been to the YMCA pool in several weeks for various reasons.

After the physical exam, she recapped what we had discussed during my visit as far as some actions I needed to take: lower my cholesterol, get a blood test, fill the prescription for my allergies.

"Oh, and I really want to see you start swimming again," Dr. Judy said with a smile as she snapped her laptop shut and shook my hand on her way out of the office. "You really *twinkled* when you talked about that."

I had to grin as I shook her hand. *Twinkled*? A medical doctor in a white lab coat actually told me that I *twinkled*?

When I thought about it later I realized that she was absolutely right. Swimming *is* one of the things that lights me up inside. Dr. Judy *was* paying attention, or she wouldn't have noticed this about me.

Because of this conversation with my new doctor, I'm back to swimming at the YMCA a couple of times a week and it feels wonderful. I'm also recommending Dr. Judy to assorted friends and family members!

I can't help thinking that it would be a very different world if medical doctors prescribed "Do what makes you twinkle" more often.

Time for Reflection

Close your eyes for a minute and see if you can remember the last time you felt all lit up (sparkly! twinkly!) on the inside. What were you doing? Who were you with? Where in your body did you feel it?

Open your eyes and make a list of things that make you twinkle. Then make a commitment to yourself to do *just one* of those things this week. If you want, make a SoulCollage® card for one of these things and journal with it to find out how you can add more twinkling light to your own life.

CHAPTER 9

Can't See For Lookin'

MY DAD NEVER took himself seriously. Sometimes when he was looking for something and it was right under his nose, he would say "I can't see for lookin'." It makes me smile even more now that I'm older, because I'm noticing lately that I also miss the obvious more often than not.

Searching the house frantically for my keys? They're usually already in my purse. Looking for my glasses so I can watch TV? Uh oh, they're pushed up on the top of my head!

When I lived in Salem, I always dreaded a certain intersection because there was no left turn and I had to turn right every time, which took me a few precious minutes out of my way. I lived there for several *years* before it finally dawned on me that even though I couldn't turn left, it didn't mean I had to turn right. I had another option and it was right in front of me the whole time: go straight!

Last fall while on vacation my gym bag zipper got jammed in a plastic bag. On arriving home, I was able to get most of the plastic out of the zipper, but the tiniest bit was still there, and no matter what I did, I couldn't zip the bag shut anymore. I was really disappointed because I love that gym bag. It's a bright shade of turquoise with white flowers and it always makes me happy to look at it.

In my struggle to unjam the zipper, I tried everything I could think of, to no avail. Then one day I went to wrestle with it and... voila! Like magic, the zipper closed. I thought it was a miracle, and was about to alert the news media when I really looked closely at the gym bag. Guess what I saw? It has *two* zippers! I'd been so busy frantically working on the zipper with the plastic stuck in it that I hadn't even noticed the other one.

Time for Reflection

Is there something that you are struggling with today? Something simple like an idea for a birthday present, or what to serve for a special dinner? Or maybe something a little more complicated, like a relationship issue or a career change?

If there is, I urge you to take some time this week to simply stop, be still and look, really look around you (on the outside *and* the inside). I can almost guarantee that the solution is right there on the border of your current vision, just waiting to be seen.

CHAPTER 10

Too Much of a Good Thing?

Too much of a good thing is wonderful.

~ MAE WEST

I FIRST STUMBLED across the above quotation when I was working in the corporate world. The words were worked brightly in cross-stitch, carefully framed, and hanging in my boss's office. She was a sophisticated woman, older than me, and truth be told, I always felt a bit intimidated in her presence. I was drawn to the quote, although I didn't exactly understand it. It seemed to deal with the areas of excess and abundance, and I was definitely not comfortable thinking about any of *that*! So I shrugged the quotation off as something that "a woman like her" would believe in.

Now I'm looking at the quote again, in the context of SoulCollage®, and I see it in a whole new light. If you've been to one of my workshops, you've probably heard me reference this passage as we approach the table where thousands of images lay spread out, waiting for new homes on SoulCollagers' cards. I say these words with a lilt in my voice, "Too much of a good thing is wonderful and that definitely includes SoulCollage® images!" Everyone usually laughs a bit, but I mean it with all my heart. Having *too many* SoulCollage® images is indeed a wonderful thing! In fact, I don't think you can ever have "enough."

It's taken me a while to get comfortable with this concept, though. When I attended my first workshop, the facilitator (Noelle) had hundreds of images and even more magazines spread out over the countertops in the little mobile trailer we were in. My soul simply *soared* at the sheer abundance of images present for my choosing. And I distinctly remember Noelle encouraging us to take more of the images and magazines home. At first I was feeling a little shy about it; I didn't want to be labeled as "greedy."

But there was a part of me who was beginning to embrace the idea of being worthy of abundance, and she won out over the part of me who thought I might be seen as greedy.

I carried as many magazines as my tote bag and arms could hold and spent a deliciously exciting and soul-satisfying evening ripping images out of those magazines.

Opening to the idea of having more than enough of a good thing has rippled outwards and spread through my life in other ways besides images for my cards. I find myself more open now to allowing myself to have what I want for myself: a huge cardboard box full of hundreds of crayons, a whole day once a week to explore my art, an hour to read a novel, an extra serving of homemade pie if I'm still hungry, or a boatload of kisses from my grandchildren.

Time for Reflection

This week, think about the concept "too much of a good thing." Meditate on the idea of abundance. In what areas of your life are you opening up and allowing excess to be a *good* thing? In what areas of your life are you blocking the flow of abundance?

Can you get in touch with the parts of your Inner Committee who are blocking this flow? Make a SoulCollage® card to honor one of them this week. Listen to its story. See if it lets up a bit and allows you to experience abundance in a new way.

CHAPTER 11

The True Meaning of Letting Go

PICTURE THIS: I'M happily settling into an airplane window seat, on my way to Buffalo on a business trip. Glancing out the window, what do I see? A baggage handler lifting *my* suitcase off the conveyer belt and carrying it back *inside* the terminal.

This is when I truly learned the meaning of *letting go*. Up until that very moment, in my early thirties, I pretty much believed that I was the one who was in control. Small things, big things. I hadn't come up against much in my life yet that required a complete and total surrender. Enter that baggage handler. Carrying *my* suitcase off of the plane.

There was nothing that I could do. Absolutely nothing. It did cross my mind to run screaming down the airplane's narrow aisle to try to get someone to stop the baggage guy, but I realized that would get me nowhere fast. So I sat back in my seat, and decided to enjoy the flight, to truly Let Go of that suitcase.

And do you know what? When I got to Buffalo, my suitcase was *already there*! Don't ask me how. This one goes into that big mysterious book of life's unanswerable questions. But it was there. I realized that it would have been there even if I'd spent that whole flight worrying and fretting about it, which I hadn't. I'm glad I enjoyed the ride instead.

Time for Reflection

Pause for a few moments right now. What is there in your life that you need to let go of? It might be something small, like the way your daughter does her homework, or something bigger, like a past relationship.

Whatever it is, picture it as my suitcase in the above story, being carried away by a uniformed "baggage handler." Realize that there is nothing you can do about it; it's being taken out of your life.

How does it feel to let it go? Breathe into that feeling, whatever it is, and don't judge it. Just allow it to be. If you feel so led, allow this story to inspire a SoulCollage® card for your deck.

CHAPTER 12

Expressing Your Passion

A WHILE BACK, my friend David invited me to see the *Stars on Ice* show at an arena in New Hampshire. He had won an eBay auction for front row seats, and I was the lucky one to go with him! Now here's the best part - the auction also included a skating lesson and backstage tour with United States Pairs Skating Champions John Zimmerman and Kyoko Ina. David has followed this pair for years, so he was in heaven.

We spent some time chatting with John and Kyoko before David began his lesson. One thing that struck me so beautifully was Kyoko's face and body when I asked her how she liked skating in pairs as opposed to skating single (which she had done for a while when she first started out).

She had been wearing her "polite face" previously; the smile was genuine but clearly the one she saved for reporters and fans. When she began answering my question, however, her entire being lit up from the inside. I don't remember exactly what she said, but she used words like *love, momentum, thrilling, trust*. Her face became open and animated; her body moved in rhythm with her words. Her joy was palpable and it bubbled over onto us. Here was a woman who was truly passionate about what she was doing, and her passion could be seen and felt by anyone in her presence.

That same week, my husband and I went to dinner at a new Indian restaurant in our town. During our meal, the owner came to our table to see if we were enjoying ourselves. We told him how we'd been eagerly waiting for the restaurant to open for several months. He responded by telling us about the process of opening the restaurant. His foreign accent was thick, so I only understood a few words of what he was saying. Nevertheless, I knew he was someone who loved his restaurant passionately and without reservation. I knew this because of the light that came into his face when he was talking about it, and because of the animation and excitement that was expressed through his body as he spoke.

As I thought of my time with Kyoko, and our conversation with the Indian restaurant owner, I was reminded once again of how important it is to feel passion in our work and to allow that passion to be expressed into the world.

Time for Reflection

What is your body saying when you talk about your work in the world? When you tell someone what you do for a living, is your joy visible? If not, why not? Are you holding the joy in, or is there no joy to express?

Explore the voices within your Committee who have something to say about your work, your joy, and your passion. Make a SoulCollage® card to honor at least one of them.

CHAPTER 13

Resisting Freedom

LAST NIGHT I noticed a large brown moth at the top of our kitchen window. He seemed to be asleep at the top of the blue and yellow curtains, wings folded inward. It crossed my mind to chase him away, but something told me to let him be.

Later that afternoon, washing some veggies for dinner, I observed that same moth sitting on the windowsill. Delicate front legs flexed, still a dry chalky brown color. The window was open and a beautiful soft sunny breeze was embracing the kitchen.

As I continued preparing the food, the moth began making small flying movements near the window. I certainly love my kitchen, but it was definitely not home to this small insect that was now so obviously ready to leave. I gently moved my hands towards him, my intention pure. He, however, did not know this, and fluttered his wings madly away from me. So I let him be.

A while later when I found him sitting on the sill again, I surprised him by cupping my hands lightly around him and moving as fast as I could towards the kitchen door, intent only on giving him his freedom. But fear gave him the power to escape my loving hands yet again. This time he flew madly around the kitchen while I stood by watching helplessly. The next time he headed towards the door, I quickly opened it and then, finally, he was free.

As I watched him soaring through the early summer sunshine, something lifted in my heart. I almost felt Spirit putting her loving hand on my shoulder, thanking me for taking the time to give this tiny sliver of Her creation its freedom.

This brought to mind several flashbacks to times in my *own* life when freedom was right in front of me, yet I resisted any loving hands that were helping me towards an open door. Memories of fears that held me back over the years fluttered through my mind as that moth had fluttered around my kitchen.

I realized that freedom is almost always right in front of us. The choice is ours. We can either allow our fear to beat so loudly in our bodies that it stops us from moving towards the freedom, or we can relax and trust in the loving Hands that are leading us to the open door.

P.S. I thought that this tiny creature was a moth because when its wings were closed, it was a dull brown color. But when I watched it rise through our backyard on the wind of its freedom, I noticed that it was a gorgeous orange and brown butterfly, not a moth at all.

Time for Reflection

Do you have a SoulCollage® card in your deck for the part of you who resists freedom because of fear or lack of faith?

Perhaps you also need one for the part of you who *does* live in faith and trust.

Each of these parts are deserving of our time and attention.

CHAPTER 14

Why Are Frogs So Happy?

THE OTHER DAY I was driving by the same town common that I pass by every week. I love this particular little patch of green because in the center of it there's a billboard announcing community events, along with a catchy quotation of some sort. Usually the words of wisdom are inspirational and educational, from famous people like Helen Keller, The Dalai Lama, and Abraham Lincoln.

Last week, in addition to an announcement about an upcoming summer concert, I saw the words *Why Are Frogs So Happy*?

Driving on, I laughingly dismissed it as simply fluff. Maybe they just couldn't think of anything else. But... guess what? I haven't been able to get that question out of my head!

Why *are* frogs so happy? And who even *thinks* about whether *frogs* are happy or not?

So far the favorite answer that's popped into my head is this: frogs are happy simply because *they are content being frogs*. Which leads me to wonder... would *I* be happier if I was content simply being *me*?

Time for Reflection

This week, think about the question "Why are frogs so happy?" as you go about your daily chores and appointments. Do you have a SoulCollage® card that addresses happiness or contentment in some way? Do you need to add one (or perhaps a frog animal totem) to your deck?

CHAPTER 15

Art of the Pause

As a self-professed self-help junkie, I've been to more than my share of lectures, workshops and retreats. I have learned oh-so-much about myself from the time I've spent in the presence of so many "gurus" of personal development and spiritual growth.

But the biggest lesson I ever learned while listening to someone else present a workshop was when the leader simply stopped talking for a minute and a half!

Yes, that's right. No words were involved in this Lesson of all Lessons.

A few years ago at Kripalu, I was participating in a session with Daniel Leven, who was leading a workshop on Body-Centered Expressive Therapy. About halfway through his presentation, someone asked a question. Whatever she asked is long gone from my memory, but I will always remember how he responded.

He simply stopped. He paused for a few seconds, looking down at the microphone he held in his hand. Then he said, "I'm sorry, I don't know exactly how to answer that. Give me a minute to get my thoughts together first." Then he set the microphone down on the floor, closed his eyes and proceeded to "think" for a full minute and a half.

I had never seen anything like this before, and I was totally amazed. As the seconds slid by, I recognized this as one of the most awakening moments of my life.

What a relief. What a blessed relief! We don't always have to have an answer. We can pause any time we need to, even if it doesn't seem "appropriate." I always thought that when someone asked me a question, I had to immediately spout forth some kind of an answer, or I would be taken less seriously. I always thought that not knowing the answer to a question was a marked sign of my own inadequacy and failure. But that day I learned otherwise.

In her book *Radical Acceptance*, Tara Brach points out that Pausing is a sacred thing. She says that it is the very first step in our own ability to embrace our lives with loving acceptance (radical as that may be!).

I believe that is what Daniel Leven was doing that day as he paused so deeply before answering the question presented to him. He was trusting in his own innate wisdom to call forth an answer to the question. He was opening his soul to the possibility of discovering an answer- for us, and for himself.

Let us all remember that when we pause, even for a few moments, we are consciously giving our souls time and space to listen. In this sacred pause, we are better able to hear all of the inner voices that go chattering on day after day, demanding our attention and draining our energy. Most importantly, when we pause, we allow time and space for Spirit to flow into and through us.

Time for Reflection

Consciously give yourself a few minutes to practice the Art of the Pause this week. Try pausing for just a few seconds every time someone asks you a question. You could try it at night before you close your eyes for sleep, or before each meal, or when you wash your face in the morning. Simply pause for several seconds and acknowledge the fact that you are pausing, that you are resting in silence, that you are quietly entering your own inner world.

Do you have any SoulCollage® cards in your deck that represent the part of you who enjoys pausing (or the part of you that doesn't?). Can you make one this week to honor that part?

SoulCollage® Example

Please visit kaleidosoul.com/inner-journeys-growth
The password for this page is grow

The topic to scroll down to is:
Pausing

CHAPTER 16

Over the Rainbow

My EXCITEMENT OVER rainbows is somewhat of a family joke. I have been late for more than one occasion because I've just had to pull my car over to the side of the road to watch a rainbow arching in the distance. We've come close to an accident or two as I've suddenly spied a rainbow out the car window and cried out (rather loudly) with delight. Once I even stopped a professor in the midst of a lecture and made the entire class come with me to the window because...you guessed it...there was a rainbow brightening the sky in the distance.

I really don't mind when people think this is odd. In fact, *I* find it rather odd when everyone else *doesn't* get excited about rainbows. It seems to me that a rainbow is an extraordinary gift from a universe that can at times be dull and obstinately predictable. I want to always be on the lookout for rainbows, and for anything that makes the ordinary into something astonishing.

Yesterday I saw a butterfly that was like a fragile piece of buttery yellow chiffon, fluttering its wings from here to there, and it made me smile. Last week our oldest granddaughter flung her arms around me and hung on for several minutes. From time to time I pause and watch the birds at the feeder in the back yard. Each of these moments is its own precious rainbow.

Time for Reflection

When you pause throughout your day today, what "rainbows" do you see? How can you consciously create a space for more rainbows to break through in your life?

Make a SoulCollage® card for the part of you who notices rainbows, or to honor someone in your life who is a rainbow-bringer.

SoulCollage® Example

Please visit kaleidosoul.com/inner-journeys-growth
The password for this page is grow

The topic to scroll down to is:
Rainbows

CHAPTER 17

Pausing on the Journey

WHILE I WAS working on the "new and improved" KaleidoSoul website in 2009, I had a chance to look back on the last five years of my life since I'd started my business. This looking back started when I began editing and re-writing the 189 pages of content that make up the heart of KaleidoSoul.com.

I found that I was remembering where I was when I wrote a certain page, how I was feeling when a particular blog entry was created. At that time, I was still using my husband's computer in his study. Two of my stepchildren were living with us and I stayed upstairs most of the time, churning out the pages, carrying my creation forward, one baby step at a time.

When I look back to 2005 and even all the way up until 2007, I realize that I had no idea how big an entity I was creating when I began building KaleidoSoul. If you're painting a huge mural that takes up the side of a building, you can only really see the little brick that's in front of you at the moment. Except, in this metaphor, I didn't even know there was a whole building attached to what I was "painting!"

I began creating KaleidoSoul simply because I wanted a place for my workshop participants (here in eastern Massachusetts) to "land" after leaving the warm safe womb of our workshop space. After a while, people from all over the world began finding KaleidoSoul online, and using it for their own safe SoulCollage® space. Little by little, brick by brick, the community began to grow. Inch by inch, baby step by baby step, I moved forward, following that little inner voice of wisdom that guided me every step of the way.

As I pause and look back, I can see my journey more clearly. I can see, in hindsight, the value of trusting that inner voice that says, "Let's try this," or "What about that?" or "What would happen if we...."

But right smack in the middle of that journey? I had no idea how far I was being taken. I had no idea what was really claiming me. I had no concept of the scope of what I was creating.

I am finding much value in pausing to take a breath as I look back over the last five years. As I was plodding along all that time, doing the daily work, writing web pages, posting messages on the KaleidoSoul Yahoo Group, and making new SoulCollage® cards, I couldn't really see where the journey was taking me.

I think this is true for all of us. Every day we put on our hiking boots or high heels (as the situation demands!) and sweep off into the details. We don't usually see the forest for the trees, as my dad used to say.

I'm not the only one who is on this amazing journey. And I *know* I'm not the only one who has made huge inner and outer strides in the last five years. Every one of us has come a long way, and maybe now is a good time for *you* to pause and look back as well.

Time for Reflection

Take some time this week to pause in the midst of *your own* journey. Look back over the last five years of your life and see what comes up for you. You might automatically think, "Nothing's changed for me. My life is the same ol' same ol'." But wait. Pause a bit longer. Play with these questions a bit. See what arises.

- Where were you five years ago? What were you doing?
- How has your outer life changed since then?
- How has your inner life changed since then?
- What part does SoulCollage® play in your life now as opposed to five years ago?

- Would you do anything differently if you could have a "do-over" on the last five years?
- What people, animals, ideas, or other resources have accompanied you on your journey during the last five years?
- Make a SoulCollage® card that represents the essence of the last five years of your own journey.
- Make a SoulCollage® Community card for someone who has played an important piece on *your* five-year journey.

CHAPTER 18

Every Picture Tells a Story

I WAS WATCHING the Robert Redford interview from *The Actor's Studio* the other day and learned something new. One of his passions has always been telling stories. He spoke of growing up with stories being an integral part of the fabric of his daily life. Stories were told to teach lessons. Bedtime stories were a given. He grew up drawing and sketching and writing stories. I didn't know this about him, even though I have a SoulCollage® card to honor his creativity and passion for the environment. It's interesting to me that Robert Redford's art informs his writing which gives him breadth as an actor and vision as a director. And all of this stems from a love of storytelling.

I gravitate towards novels and films that tell deep, passionate stories about real human beings. Plays and musicals thrill me when they burn to tell a powerful emotional story. *Aida, Les Miserables, Into the Woods,* and *Kiss of the Spider Woman* are good examples.

To me, a "good" piece of art tells a story too. Look at your favorite painting, your most-loved photograph, your most treasured SoulCollage® card. Are there not stories there? And are those stories not medicine for your soul? They are indeed medicine that soothes the spirit the way aspirin and a cool wash cloth soothe a headache. Medicine that takes our twisted journeys and straightens them into magnificent things of light and truth, stories worth loving and sharing.

Time for Reflection

What story does your favorite SoulCollage® card tell about you, about your journey on this earth?

Who can you share that story with today?

How does the story of your life show in your art?

Do you have a card in your deck for *your* favorite storyteller?

SoulCollage® Example:

Please visit kaleidosoul.com/inner-journeys-growth

Password: grow

The topic to scroll down to is:

Robert Redford

CHAPTER 19

Every, Every Minute

Goodbye world, goodbye Grover's Corners, Mama and Papa.
Goodbye to ticking clocks and my butternut tree and mama's
sunflowers, food and coffee, new ironed dresses and hot
baths and sleeping and waking up. Oh earth, you're too wonderful for anybody to realize you. Do any human beings ever
realize life while they live it- every, every minute?

~ Thornton Wilder

I was only 14 years old when I first heard these words from the magnificent play *Our Town*. I was too young to have made any acquaintance
with death but I intuitively knew that Emily's soliloquy held the key to
the entire meaning of life. As I heard the actress on the stage say these
lines, I grandly resolved that I was going to live my life differently. I was
going to notice every, *every* minute of my life. When the end of my life
came, I was not going to look back and realize I'd lived too quickly, or
that I'd not participated in my life fully.

But then of course, my life went flying forward and filled up with
homework assignments and afternoon club meetings, college applications, dates and appointments. I forgot about the play and those words
that had so deeply touched my heart. There were times when I paused,
when I stood still and looked at the sky, but those times were terribly few,
and for the most part, Emily's words were forgotten.

Once in a while I am reminded, though. I'll see *Our Town* on television, or I'll see this quotation used in another context, and then I will stop and remember. Ah, yes. *This* is what life is s all about.

I stop then, and I look around me. I take in the wonder of a darkening night sky, the cheerful way my cat swaggers up the sidewalk, the pretty freckles on my granddaughter's nose. I pause and listen to my heartbeat, smell the lilacs on a summer breeze, taste the cool water as it tickles my tongue. It's *all* important, every last bit of it.

Time for Reflection

Stop for a moment right now and look around you. What do you notice about this life you are living? What do you want to remember about *this* moment?

Set an intention to live life to its fullest *every, every minute.*

Make a list of the sights, sounds, smells, tastes, and touches that you love.

Make a SoulCollage® card for the part of you that embraces life fully. Or make a card that reflects your new intention. Place it where it will serve as a daily reminder to pay attention.

CHAPTER 20

Holes

I'VE BEEN DRAWN lately to thinking about the empty places, the holes inside of me. Where are they? Why are they empty? Is it okay to have empty spaces inside of me? How do I try to fill them? Can I let the emptiness just be, or do I have to fill it with something? What are the hurtful ways that I fill the emptiness? What are some good, more life-giving ways to fill it?

Meditating on this for several days in a row, I have named a few of the empty places inside of me:

- The hole that is the children I never had
- The holes that are the three women friends who moved away and left me behind
- The hole where my three beloved cats used to be

Sometimes life digs holes inside of us. It is hard to accept these empty spaces. Peering into them sometimes makes me feel like I am swallowing acid: a sharp burning in my eyes, my throat, my spirit.

But there are also holes inside of me that I dug myself. These are hollow, vacant places that I have created of my own volition. These are unintentional holes, but nonetheless they are there:

- The hole where my art practice used to be
- Holes of hurt and indignation
- Empty places of longing and regret

And I wonder... can a hole also be an opening? If I am brave enough to enter the cold vacant craters of my own soul, can I find some clarity and ease in their emptiness? Can I be courageous enough to sit inside one of these holes and either accept its presence in my life just as it is or discern what I might need to fill it?

Here are the destructive things I try to fill my holes with: too much television, internet surfing, junk food, sugar, tasteless food. And here are the life-giving "fillings" that remind me that I am already whole: writing, art, dance, long walks, time with those I love, playing with cats, theatre, music, the ocean.

Time for Reflection

Identify some of the "holes" in your own life. Can you explore these empty spaces without judgment, without trying to fill them up?

What destructive things do you use to fill the holes in your soul?

What life-giving things can you use to fill them instead?

Make a SoulCollage® card to express your hole-y holy self.

CHAPTER 21

Telling All Your Heart

IN HER BOOK *The Gifts of Imperfection*, Brené Brown talks about the qualities that make up what she calls a Wholehearted Life. One of these qualities is courage. Did you know that the root of the word "courage" is cor, which is the Latin word for "heart?" The original meaning of the word courage is *"to speak one's mind by telling all one's heart."* Isn't that just beautiful?

Brené says that nowadays we tend to get heroics confused with ordinary courage. We tend to think of "heroes" as the only ones who are courageous. Of course they are, and this is because they have put their lives on the line. Think of the bystander who dives into the water to save a drowning child. Think of the firefighters on September 11. Think of the one who runs into a burning building to save a woman's beloved dog.

Yet they are not the only ones who exemplify courage.

I thought a lot about courage when I was going through my surgeries and treatments for cancer in 2002. Friends often commented on how "courageous" I was and that puzzled me because I felt anything but courageous. I was full of fear, but from listening to my friends, I learned that the act of actually *navigating* that fear instead of giving in to it was another true meaning of courage.

For me, that really was a *choice*, and as Brené explains in her book, it was a real example of putting my vulnerability on the line by allowing the fear, accepting it, living side by side with it, and ultimately learning to navigate it.

Recently, I was participating in a committee meeting and we were trying to come to consensus on a certain matter. It seemed like we were all in agreement but at the last moment, one woman spoke up and told us why she wasn't in agreement with us. That was a heroic, courageous thing to do. It turns out that because she *spoke her mind by telling us her heart*, this opened up a brand new dialogue, and we were able to come to an even better decision than we had thought possible at the beginning.

I am making my way through my days now, looking for ways to truly speak my mind and "tell my heart." I know that it's not always safe to do this, and part of caring for myself is knowing when to open up and when not to.

Time for Reflection

Make a SoulCollage® card for the part of you who is courageous in matters of the heart.

Pay attention when people in your life speak their mind and their heart in courageous ways.

Make a SoulCollage® Community card for one of these people and let it be a visual reminder for you to do the same.

Make a commitment this week to (just *one* time) speak up exactly what you are thinking and feeling, even though it might go against the flow of expectations. Be sure that you are in a safe environment, with people who are open to your truth. Watch what happens!

CHAPTER 22

Stopping to Smell the Snowbanks

WINTER WALKS WITH Suzy, our yellow lab, have been fraught with frustration for me. She's always stopping to sniff around dirty snowbanks, among other things. As the bitter wind whips around my frozen cheeks, I keep trying to urge her on, to keep moving. What's going on in my mind is this, "Come on; it's freezing out here. That's just a filthy snowbank; what could possibly interest you there?"

Then one morning on such a walk, I realized something important, something that put an end to my frustration. My dog knows waaaaaaay more about being in the present moment than I do. I discovered that she was approaching the walk from a totally different perspective. I was looking at it as time to *walk*, and she was looking at it as just *time*.

Ever since then, I've been much more mindful throughout these daily walks. I've made an agreement with myself to pause several times, or at least once on each street we encounter. And no, I'm not pausing to admire the dirty snowbanks. I have been known to stop still in the middle of the street and gaze upwards at the astonishing beauty of a perfect V formation of honking geese. Today I stopped completely under a towering tree and breathed in deeply that intoxicating fresh scent of wet pine. Yesterday I paused at the end of our driveway and took in our beautiful home, offering prayers of gratitude as I did so.

And yes, sometimes Suzy is pulling at the leash when I am taking my pauses. But I figure that if I have to wait while she pauses to admire something that fascinates *her*, then *she* can wait a moment for *me* too. There's so much in our wide beautiful world that can be fascinating, if only I stop to admire it and breathe it in.

I am hoping that after a few months of this new practice while on my daily walk, this pausing will transfer over into the rest of my day as well. To stop and just stand (or sit) still a few times, even if only for thirty seconds, in the midst of a busy day... what a concept! As Arthur Rubenstein so eloquently said, "I handle the notes no better than many others, but the pauses- ah! that is where the art resides."

Time for Reflection

Try to incorporate at least two very brief pauses into each day this week, even if for only fifteen seconds at a time. It's not as easy to remember to do this as it sounds, so you might want to post some notes around to remind yourself.

Make a SoulCollage® card for the part of you who longs to "stop and smell the snowbanks" on your way through life. Ask him or her how you can slow down and enjoy your life more.

SoulCollage® Resources:

To help you remember to pause throughout your day, try using the Remindfulness App. remindfulnessapp.com

Another helpful way to assist you with your pausing is the Meaning to Pause bracelet, which looks beautiful on your wrist and vibrates gently every hour as a peaceful reminder. meaningtopause.com

CHAPTER 23

This Is Your Life and It Is Precious

> For you created my inmost being;
> you knit me together in my mother's womb.
> I praise you because I am fearfully and wonderfully made;
> your works are wonderful,
> I know that full well.
>
> ~ PSALM 139

A BIG PART of my life story is my relationship with Dan who was an alcoholic. Because of that relationship, I found myself going to lots of 12 Step meetings. This significantly changed my spiritual journey such that I was strengthened and enabled to grow in ways that I had never thought possible.

The biggest turning point for me in this growth was when I did the Fifth Step, which reads: *Admitted to God, myself, and another human being, the exact nature of my wrongs.*

To do this Step, I spent hours and hours creating a list of my "liabilities." These could also be called flaws, or in SoulCollage® lingo, "shadow parts." Believe me, I had a loooooong list, about two-and-a-half pages, typed, single spaced. I also spent many hours writing my whole life story up until that point, and it was laden with mistakes I'd made, regrets, and sorrow.

The final part of preparation for this Step was to create a list of my personal "assets," inner characteristics that I liked about myself. This list? Let's just say that it didn't even fill up half a page.

Looking inward like this was not the most difficult part of this Step. The hardest part (for me, anyway) was to sit down with "another human being" and share all of it. I chose Randy, the Episcopal priest at the church I was attending then. He was familiar with 12 Step programs, and he was absolutely the safest person I knew at that time.

With much anxiety and fear, I sat down with Randy one spring morning in 1988. I had never done anything like this before - shared my entire life story, my lists of good and bad, with another person.

At one point while I was telling my story, I paused and apologized for going on and on about a really difficult part of my journey. Randy gently responded, "That's okay. This is your life and it is very precious." No one had ever said anything like that to me before. Ever. I was stunned into a holy silence for a while! In fact, I had never been *listened* to like this before. While I was talking, he simply and actively *listened* to every word I said. It was powerful and healing simply to be heard and seen in this way. I realized later that this is the highest form of validation- being listened to with such concentration and acceptance.

After about an hour and a half of telling my story and listing the parts of myself I did not like, Randy asked about my "assets." I read them to him and it took all of two minutes. Then he took the pages of my life story and my shadow parts away from me. He nodded towards the list of assets that were still in my hands, then told me to go home and:

a.   Give thanks to God for my assets
b.   Meditate on Psalm 139
c.   Thank God for my life and for my journey

At first I was confused, annoyed, and even a bit disappointed. I had thought we were going to sit there and *discuss* all of the mistakes I had made. I thought he was going to give me wise counsel and advice on how I could make my liabilities *disappear.* Instead, I was being told to go home and focus on my positive qualities, offer thanksgiving, and meditate on a Psalm that I had never heard of.

Here's what happened: I did exactly what he said. And my life has never been the same.

Time for Reflection

Make a list (long or short) of your own personal inner "assets."

Thank God (or Source, Spirit, The One, Allah...) for these assets.

Meditate for a while on Psalm 139.

Make a SoulCollage® card that visually expresses the concept of this Psalm.

Make a list of the mistakes, losses, regrets, and wrong turns that you've made on your journey so far. Next, add to the list all of the joys, blessings, and bright things that have happened to you.

Note which list is longer but please *do not judge* any of it! Go somewhere quiet, hold the lists gently in your hands and slowly say (preferably out loud) ten times, "This is my life and it is very precious."

CHAPTER 24

Mystery Ingredients

A WHILE BACK I became seriously attached (that's my euphemism for *addicted!*) to a Food Network show called *Chopped* where four professional chefs are given a basket of "mystery ingredients" and challenged to create an appetizer, entrée, or dessert.

For example, in one episode they had to make a dessert using boxed macaroni and cheese, apples, raw cashews and cane syrup. Another time they were given short ribs, lemon thyme, zucchini and gummy bears, and challenged to create an entrée. Can you possibly imagine what kind of appetizer you'd come up with if you were given peanut butter, granny smith apples, and bacon?

Each menu item is judged on presentation, taste, and creative use of the ingredients. In each round, the judges taste all of the chefs' food and say what they think. After everyone has had their say, they hold a discussion and agree on which chef is to be "chopped" from the competition. After three rounds, there is only one chef still standing and he or she is the winner.

Every time I look at the mystery ingredients, I am positively certain that they won't be able to come up with something edible that looks good on the plate. And every time... every single time, I am proven wrong.

It reminds me of when I was teaching second grade. I sometimes gave my students an assignment of combining unrelated spelling words into a sentence. For example, dime-lines-sky. Or dinner-thumb-bells. The sentences those kids came up with always amazed me! It required a different way of looking at the words and using them out of context. I like to think that this challenge helped my students with their creative thinking skills later on in life as well.

The theme of mystery ingredients also reminds me of Paper Bag Dramatics, a fun game we used to play when I was a Girl Scout. The leaders would bring in four paper bags, each containing several unrelated items. A bag might include a toothbrush, framed photo, book of maps, shawl, piece of chalk, broken radio and ball of yarn. Each group of girls was given a different bag of props and the challenge was to come up with a ten minute skit using all of the items. I loved this game because it brought about much laughter and playfulness as we tried to think of possible creative ways to thread these items into a plausible story.

So . . . back to *Chopped*. I love this show the way I loved Paper Bag Dramatics, and the way I loved challenging my students to combine their unrelated spelling words into interesting sentences because it reminds me of the power of creativity in our everyday lives.

Also, I can relate this show to the *larger* mysteries of life. At any given point on our journey, we are being handed a bag of "ingredients," and let me tell you, some of them are more mysterious than others. For instance, right now, my Life Ingredients include a loving husband, grief work for Lis and Sasha, a growing business/work that I love, and chemo treatments that are sapping my energy. How do I combine these four things into my life in a way that brings me balance and inner peace? How do these mystery ingredients come together to make meaning, to activate growth, to bring me closer to myself, others, and Spirit?

Time for Reflection

Stop this week and take a step back from your life.

Make a list of the main "Mystery Ingredients" that are on your plate right now.

Keep your list out where you can see it often.

What are some ways that you can work with all of these "ingredients" you've been given in order to bring about more growth and meaning in your life?

Do a reading with your SoulCollage® deck to help you sort out some answers to the above question.

And relax! Unlike in *Chopped*, no one is judging you. It's all about noticing, being aware, and falling in love with yourself over and over again.

SoulCollage® Resources

Visit KaleidoSoul.com/cardreadings for more info about the readings process.

Listen to Seena B. Frost's CD *Doing Readings with SoulCollage®*.

CHAPTER 25

Permission Slips

WHEN I WAS in high school, if we wanted to go to the library during study hall, or to the bathroom during a regular class, we had to get a permission slip from the teacher. The assumption was that unless we had specific permission, we *didn't have the right* to be walking out in the empty hallways during scheduled class time. Now, since I'm much older and maybe a little wiser, I am starting to think that I might still need a permission slip from time to time, to encourage me to step out of the boundaries I've locked myself into for so long.

According to the dictionary, "permission" means *authorization granted to do something*. In high school, that authority came from the teacher or principal. Nowadays, I am realizing that *I* (and I alone) am the one who has this authority over my life.

So I am asking myself (and I invite you to do the same) these questions in relation to permission:

- What don't I believe I *have the right* (or the time or the talent) to do?
- What rules have I been following that don't exist anymore except in my mind?
- What am I stopping myself from doing that would ultimately bring me joy? Why?

For me, the answers to these questions vary from day to day, and month to month. They will vary for you as well, and from year to year, and decade to decade. Lately I seem to be telling myself I don't have the time to doodle in my art journal, make new collages, and play with paint on the artist canvases I've been stockpiling.

So I've decided to write myself some daily Permission Slips. My Permission Slip today reads: *I give myself permission to spend thirty minutes this afternoon at my art table with my crayons, paints, and markers.* I print my Permission Slips onto pretty colored paper, and I always sign and date them. If signing them with your own name seems a bit too difficult right now, you could sign them from one of your more encouraging, supportive Neters.

Either way, I encourage you this week and in the weeks ahead to take a look at the areas of your life where giving yourself gentle permission could be just the thing you need to break out of an old rut or habit.

Time for Reflection

Create your own blank Permission Slips. Feel free to add embellishments, graphics, stickers, doodles, or whatever makes you smile when you look at them.

Journal for a while with the three questions above.

Write yourself one permission slip each week this month. Be sure to sign and date it, and place it somewhere you'll see it often during the day.

CHAPTER 26

Choice Anxiety

AT OUR LATEST KaleidoSoul Retreat, I decided to spend some time making cards. I sat down on the floor, spread out my many images, and squooshed them together in little piles according to my own themes. Then I just sat, looking at them in confusion. There were 15-20 piles in all. Where on earth should I begin?

Another SoulCollager walked by me just then and must have noticed the perplexed look on my face. "Experiencing a little choice anxiety?" she murmured in good humor.

I was so excited; what I was feeling had a name! This comforted me a great deal, so much so that I was able to get past the fact that I had an overwhelming plethora of wonderful choices in front of me. I was finally able to tune in to which pile I really wanted to explore first.

Ever since that day, I've noticed this phenomenon repeating itself in my life in many different situations. The library: so many books, so little time. My art table: should I paint or collage or play with my crayons? My writing: which project do I delve into first? The drug store: which kind of toothpaste will I buy? A restaurant: which mouthwatering selection do I want to eat right now? The openness of a day off: what will I do with all this time?

When faced with so many options, I often become overwhelmed. It's just too much. A lot of times I feel so inundated with choices that I end up not choosing anything! I've decided that for me, this is not a healthy response, so I've been looking for ways to break through the paralysis that so many options incur.

So many choices. Most of them good. When faced with this anxiety-producing perplexity of positive options, I try to remember to get quiet on the outside so I can hear my own sweet voice of wisdom on the inside. I've noticed that when I do this, the anxiety simply melts away and the choice is made clear.

Time for Reflection

Are there any areas in your life where "choice anxiety" is getting in your way?

What Committee parts have something to say about the possibility of having so many wonderful options in front of you?

Listen carefully . . . you will get some great clues as to how to deal with your own "choice anxiety."

CHAPTER 27

Face to Face

WHILE VISITING US at Christmas last year, our granddaughter Tori toddled up to a large mirror that was resting against our sofa. She immediately knelt down and greeted her own image with the sweetest of kisses.

I keep this photo on my desk now for two reasons:

1. Our granddaughter is beloved beyond measure and the sight of her makes me smile.
2. It is a welcome reminder of how I want to greet and embrace my own precious self whenever I have the opportunity.

Time for Reflection

Pause for a moment the next time you walk by a mirror.

Stand face to face with yourself. Look yourself in the eye.

Touch hands with yourself in acknowledgement of how wonderful and precious you are.

Go ahead and give yourself a little kiss!

CHAPTER 28

Holding This Moment in My Hand

THE FRENCH WORD for "now" is "maintenant," which literally means "held in the hand." I like this word because it's a gentle reminder that I am holding *this* moment, right now, in my hand. This moment is all that I have.

As I type these words onto this blank computer screen, I am holding a moment in my hand. As I close my eyes and hear the sounds of a house quieting down for the night . . . I am holding a moment in my hand. Every time I hear our grandchildren laugh . . . I hold a moment in my hand. Whenever I look to the sky, cross a crowded street, or sneeze . . . I am holding a moment in my hand.

One of my intentions this year is to be more present to my own life as it is unfolding, moment by moment. It is my spiritual responsibility to savor all of these moments, one at a time, as they are given to me. Even on days when I would rather turn my back on them, I am going to try to remember that they are gifts from the One who loves me more than I could ever love myself.

I am going to try to savor each moment. I am going to try to hold this moment in my hand. Maintenant. Now. The only moment that I have.

Time for Reflection
Create a personal intention related to the word *maintenant*.

Create a SoulCollage® card that expresses your intention, or choose a card that you already have.

Keep your intention card on your desk or bedside table where you can see it often.

Allow it to speak to you this week. Have a conversation with it. What are you learning about holding this moment in your hand?

CHAPTER 29

What I Learned While Riding the Metro

SEVERAL YEARS AGO, my husband and I spent a delightful week in Washington D.C. After visiting Jeff's brother a few hours west of the city, and then bopping around Williamsburg, a few hours south of the city, we ditched our rental car and journeyed on the Metro. What a fabulous experience! Besides being shiny clean, remarkably fast, and easy to follow, it became for me a lesson in life and living. Here's what I learned:

1. **Hold on lightly and relax** - After just a few minutes of standing up on our first Metro ride,

I realized how tense I was. My knees were locked; I was clinging for dear life to the shiny silver pole. Then I noticed a young boy, about eight years old. He was standing, but he wasn't holding on to anything! I admired him for a bit, still hanging on as tightly as I could. Then I realized that he was remaining steady and he wasn't falling over. *No one* else was falling over either. So I loosened my grip on the pole, relaxed my shoulders and legs, and just went with the flow of the ride. Believe me, it was a much more pleasant way to travel.

2. **Strangers aren't really strangers** - A gleaming silver train pulled up while we were waiting for one on a different track, and I witnessed something that will always stay with me as a reminder of how we are all connected. A business man was running to catch the train. He started to

step into the passenger car just as the doors began to close, and then his briefcase got stuck in the grip of the shiny metallic doors while he remained on the platform. He looked around desperately, determined not to let go of his briefcase. Then suddenly, from nowhere it seemed, six people rushed over to help him pry open the doors. He didn't even call out for help. They were just *there*. And they weren't all Caucasian businessmen like him, either. There were two women who had just finished a workshop, an African-American man, and another dark-skinned man with a turban. A few of them were in jeans and well-worn t-shirts. A few others were dressed professionally. One of them looked like he was heading out for a night at the Opera. And they all helped, no questions asked.

3. **All it takes is a smile** - We were taking a late train back to our hotel after a comedy show downtown. There was no one else in our section except a young man, shabbily dressed, sitting alone. His hair was unkempt and even though one of my inner voices was trying to incite me to fear, I felt drawn to him. He spent the whole ride looking down at a book that he held in his hands, but I could see that he wasn't really reading it. When Jeff and I stood up to get off at our stop, I bravely made eye contact with him, and we both smiled at the same time. I know I will never see him again, but for just that moment a smile struck a connection between us that was both rare and beautiful.

Time for Reflection

Try letting go of something you've been clutching too tightly and see if your ride through life is any easier.

Notice the good in the people around you.

Smile at a stranger.

What lessons have you learned in your own life that you could express with a SoulCollage® card? Why not make one this week?

CHAPTER 30

It Is What It Is

You don't need no license for how you be feeling.
What it is,
is what it is.

~ ELIZABETH CUNNINGHAM,
THE RETURN OF THE GODDESS: A DIVINE COMEDY

THESE PROFOUND WORDS are spoken by a character named Marvin in Elizabeth Cunningham's achingly wise and beautiful novel of a woman growing into her own soul. Marvin is not someone who appears on the outside to be capable of great wisdom. He has little education, a prison record, and no steady job. Yet he does possess something that allows him to be a channel for the divine to flow through him; he has a deep knowledge and certain acceptance of who he is.

I love this quotation because it reminds me on a deep level that feelings are a part of who I am. When I get to know my feelings, I have a better knowing of who I am on many levels. The more I accept my feelings, the more I open up space inside of me for the Divine to flow through me to others.

My feelings are *mine*. They are part of *who I am*, part of my divine interior wiring. On any given day, these emotions may be pleasant or unpleasant, complex or simple, welcome or unwelcome, soothing or hurtful. This quotation reminds me of the simple fact that all of these emotions are *mine*. Each one is a precious fragment of my unique soul.

Time for Reflection

I once saw a bumper sticker that said IT IS WHAT IT IS. It resonated so clearly with me that I immediately went home, printed it out in several fonts, and placed it in strategic places around our house where I would be sure to see it every day. Do the same thing for yourself. Place these words, or Marvin's words above, where you will often be reminded to accept your feelings as they are, however they present themselves to you.

Make a list of every emotion that you've experienced in the past month.

Create a SoulCollage® card this month that honors a feeling from your list.

CHAPTER 31

Inner Beauty

AT THE END of a weekend retreat I once attended, we were each given a hand mirror and instructed to gaze into our own eyes for several minutes. I had never done that before, and I have to admit it was simply breathtaking!

Think about it. When you're standing in front of the mirror brushing your teeth or checking to see how your outfit looks, how many times have you actually *looked into your own eyes?*

At the retreat, after looking into our eyes for several minutes, we were asked to write a love letter to ourselves. I still have that love letter and I still read it out loud to myself every few months.

I also still enjoy the feeling of self-empowerment and of truly connecting with myself that accompanied this exercise. When I look into my own eyes like this, I am reminded once again of who I really am: a woman full of beauty and light.

Time for Reflection

Clear a quiet space and time for yourself this week. Spend several minutes looking into your own eyes in a mirror. Make a ritual out of this activity if you choose. Light a candle. Play some of your favorite music. Drape a colorful scarf around your neck.

Then, write a love letter to yourself. Remind yourself of who you really are, and of all the things you find beautiful and amazing about yourself. Seal the letter and mail it to yourself. Or send it to a friend who lives far away and ask him or her to mail it to you sometime in the future when you least expect it. Another option is to frame your love letter and hang it where you'll see it often. Read it out loud to yourself once a week.

Make a SoulCollage® card that expresses the way you feel when you look into your own eyes. Use a photograph of yourself on this very important card and keep it in your deck always.

CHAPTER 32

Lit From Within

I ATTENDED A retreat once where the facilitator spent an entire afternoon with us on this question: *What lights you up?* At first I was bored with this idea. After all, I knew what things I enjoyed doing. I couldn't imagine the purpose of focusing on this for several hours. But to my chagrin, that is exactly what we did!

We each made a list of what lit us up on the inside. *What gives you the deepest joy? What makes you feel happy and delighted to be living?* My list was rather long and I was surprised that I could fill up an entire sheet of notebook paper. Then the retreat leader asked us to circle the five things on the list that we did on a regular basis. I was astonished when I realized that I couldn't circle *one* thing, not to mention *five* of them.

It turned out that I was not alone, and the rest of that afternoon was spent figuring out why we were denying ourselves these pleasures and what we could do to incorporate at least a few of them back into our daily lives.

I still have that first list I made. It reminds me that life is about so much more than the outer parts of me that the world generally sees: the doing, the producing, the accomplishing. My life is also about the *inner* me, and about giving myself those things that *light me up* inside so that the darkness of overdoing and overachieving is balanced with the joyful light that indicates the real me is at home.

Time for Reflection

What lights you up? Make a list of *at least* twenty things that fill your heart, body, and soul with joy and a feeling of being deeply centered.

Are you doing any of them on a regular, consistent basis?

What keeps you from actively pursuing these things? Take a look through your SoulCollage® deck to see if any of the darker, shadowy Neters have something to say about your list.

Choose one thing from your list and commit to doing it today and tomorrow.

Which of the other things on your list would you most like to incorporate into this coming month? Make a plan that allows you to do this.

How do you feel when you are "lit up" from the inside?

CHAPTER 33

The Difference That Praise Makes

It wasn't *American Idol*, but there I was on a Sunday afternoon, sitting with the other "judges" at a long table in the chilly basement of our local community house. The table was littered with checklists, notebooks, assorted water bottles, and various colored pens. We were auditioning young women for the roles of Meg, Jo, Beth, and Amy for our theatre group's upcoming production of *Little Women*. At the table with me were the director, co-director, stage manager, music director, and choreographer.

One by one, the girls stood in front of us, handed their sheet music to the pianist, and proceeded to sing a song of their own choosing. They ranged in age from 11-25. Some of them had all the confidence of an *American Idol* winner. But many of them did not. The more confident girls were able to light up the small space with their voices. It was quite impressive to see and hear. On the other end of the spectrum, the insecure girls were literally and metaphorically shaking in their boots, and because of this they fell completely flat.

This is when I noticed something even more impressive than the way the more confident girls sang.

Our director, Myriam, has a very patient, gentle way about her. I had been aware of this the year before when I worked backstage with her during our production of *Sound of Music*. But I'd never seen her in action during a round of auditions before!

When a girl's nerves got the best of her and she sang poorly, Myriam would stand up at the end of the audition and smile genuinely at her. "That was wonderful! You have such a sweet voice. Now, let's try it again

75

and this time could you please _____?" and she proceeded to fill in the blank with a helpful suggestion about how the girl could improve.

At first I was baffled, amused, and ultimately curious. I was thinking to myself, "Should she really be *lying* to these girls?" But then I kept on observing. After seeing several of these "bad" auditions in a row, I realized something very impressive indeed. As Myriam praised each girl, even when they had done poorly, they relaxed. I could literally *see* their bodies loosen and stand taller. They smiled. They breathed more deeply. And then what happened next is that they sang more fully, more beautifully, and more on key! They sang more like themselves.

It happened over and over again that afternoon. We were there for six hours and more than twenty girls auditioned during that time. More than half of them were nervous, insecure, and frightened; they gave a lousy first performance. But as soon as Myriam complimented them and smiled so kindly at them, their posture changed, and their mindset seemed to change along with it. As a result, their performance was remarkably better. Many of them even made it through to callbacks because of this!

And a few of them actually got parts in the show.

I marveled at this on the short drive home. *What if I talked to myself that way when I'm nervous and insecure about something in my own life? What if I took the time to smile at myself and give myself some inner encouragement, the way Myriam did with those girls?*

Since then I've been much more aware of how I'm talking to myself. I've been in several situations since then where a little inner praise has made a huge difference in my own "performance." I love knowing that I am my own inner "director" and that I have the power to influence change in all of my inner "actors."

Time for Reflection

Think about an area of your life where you could use some praise and encouragement from your own "inner director."

The next time you notice yourself feeling down, discouraged, or insecure about something, call up that kind and gentle inner director. Activate some praise for yourself. Watch what happens!

Create a SoulCollage® card for this inner director. Journal with this part of you and allow it to encourage you gently day by day, no matter what.

CHAPTER 34

Inner Adventures of the Finest Kind

I HAVE NEVER considered myself an "adventurer." To me, the word *adventure* calls to mind dangerous and risky experiences. Friends in high school would go off on wilderness camping expeditions, climbing to the top of Mt. Katahdin in Maine, and I would send them off with a happy wave. I read about people diving into deep oceans or flinging themselves out of airplanes and find myself thankful that I am not called to adventures like that.

I have never felt called to *that* kind of adventure. But recently, on a trip to Alaska, I discovered that there are *other* kinds of adventures that I *am* drawn to.

The dictionary describes *adventure* this way: *involvement in bold undertakings: the participation or willingness to participate in things that involve uncertainty and risk.* And while it's true that I don't have an inner Neter who longs for risky hikes or dives or high jumps, I do have an *Inner* Adventurer who isn't afraid of uncertain journeys with unknown outcomes.

My cruise from Seattle to Alaska in July of 2014 was an amazing adventure for both myself and my husband. I wasn't thinking of it as an actual adventure until about halfway through when our ship turned slowly into a magnificent fjord known as Tracey Arm (near Juneau). Only a mile wide and 28 miles long, this fjord had been carved by a glacier centuries ago.

Standing outside on the deck of our cabin at 5 a.m., I was overcome by the wide silence that engulfed me. The ship glided along so very slowly at 9 mph, and all around me was nothing but raw untouched mountains, waterfalls, cliffs, and wilderness. For four hours we glided up this fjord and back. The deeper we went into it, the quieter it got. It wasn't just the slowing down of the ship's engines. A deeper stillness pervaded. Even though I could see many others standing out on their own little balconies, all of us were silent.

At one point I sat down in the deck chair to rest, but it was all too raw, too precious, too majestic, and I had to stand up again. What I was feeling reminded me of being in church when everyone is expected to stand up for the Important Parts. I remained standing for the whole four hours.

There was a wonderful naturalist on board our ship, Brent Nixon, an adventurous man in his fifties who had kayaked up this fjord many times in his younger days. He had also explored most of Alaska via foot and kayak. He had done some presentations on Alaska and wildlife from the ship's main stage the day before. A high energy presenter, he often used music, expressive body movement and humor to entertain as well as teach. It was also part of his job during these cruises to narrate the Tracey Arm journey from the ship's PA system. I was a little leery of this, given the silence all around us and the sacredness of the place, but Brent didn't disappoint. He used a quiet, reverent voice to talk about the history of the fjord and what we were seeing. He spoke for ten minutes and then left us to the silence for ten minutes, and the presentation alternated like that throughout the four hours. During his narrations, he wove in quotes from Helen Keller, the Dalai Lama, Einstein, and more.

Brent also shared some quotations from his own kayaking journals. This was my favorite, and it moved me to tears:

We don't do these adventures to escape life,
We do them so that life doesn't escape us.

I raced back inside the cabin, wrote these words carefully in my journal, and pondered them as we continued gliding down the Tracey Arm. It was at that moment that I found my own definition of "adventure" changing.

Was seeing Alaska from the inside of a luxury cruise ship an adventure? I had not thought so. I previously had thought that only hiking my way through Alaska or even sky diving over Alaska could be counted as an "adventure." To go there on a lavish cruise ship actually seemed kind of wimpy to me!

But I realized something right there on our little balcony overlooking the Tracey Arm Fjord. I had wanted to go to Alaska since hearing John Denver talk and sing about it in the early 90's. In 2012, when I was recovering from chemotherapy and two major surgeries, I realized that it was time to make that particular dream a reality. I feel incredibly grateful that my husband and I were able to make it happen. And yes indeed, it was an *Adventure*! Maybe not the kind of adventure that involves incredible physical risk, but I now see that there are other kinds of adventures.

Traveling across the beautiful USA, spending a few days in Seattle, then cruising up through Alaska indeed counts as an adventure. So does absolutely *anything* I do that contains new vistas, or a reframing of old vistas. Creating a website, planning a workshop, painting backgrounds in my art journal: all of these count as adventures. Going to the grocery store or taking a class at a local community college can be an adventure, if I allow it to be! And what about my SoulCollage® practice? This is definitely an inner Adventure with a capital A.

The word Adventure now holds new meaning for me. Big or small, long or short, an adventure involves seeing new sights, revisioning old sights, meeting new people, listening on the inside, attempting inner and outer journeys with uncertain outcomes, and choosing to make a longtime dream come true.

Time for Reflection

Spend some time this week pondering the concept of Adventure. Think back on your life and write about some adventures you have had.

Do you have an adventurous spirit? Are you open to taking risks and doing things that have "uncertain outcomes?" If so, create a SoulCollage® committee card for this part of you. Allow it to speak to you of what it wants and needs from you right now in your life.

If, like me, you've never considered yourself to be adventurous, what about *inner* explorations like journaling and art and guided imagery? Those, too, count as adventures! You might consider creating a card for your own Inner Adventurer.

Journal with the Brent Nixon quote above. Have any of your *own* life's adventures served to keep life from escaping you? How so?

CHAPTER 35

What I Learned in Traffic Court

A FEW MONTHS ago I was the defendant in a seven-person jury trial from an accident that I had caused two years before. I rear ended another car going 15 mph on a main street the next town over. I had fully accepted responsibility in accident reports for the police as well as for both insurance companies. But the woman who was driving the other car decided to sue me (and my insurance company) for $9,000 worth of Physical Therapy bills and lost pay from a month when she supposedly couldn't go to work. My insurance company refused to settle because they thought the damage I'd done was not that serious.

In the days and weeks leading up to the trial, I was understandably nervous. Okay, I was downright anxious. At some point I realized that I was going to have to find a way to calm myself down or I wouldn't be able to testify on my own behalf. I did some EFT Tapping which cleared my mind so I could remember a good way to deal with a difficult/challenging situation. The result? I decided to see what I could learn from the whole "day in court" experience.

Keeping an open, inquisitive mind did wonders for my nerves and it also made me curious about the whole process. I stayed very present with myself and paid attention to everything that was happening- from arriving and meeting my insurance company's lawyer, to the jovial chitchat with the bailiff and court clerk before the judge joined us.

Because I was able to stay present with myself, I noticed how profoundly moved I was when the large pool of potential jury members walked into our courtroom. I could feel a lump in my throat and tears stinging my eyes a couple of different times throughout that long morning, and every time, it involved some aspect of the jury. There were men and women of all colors, shapes, ages, and backgrounds. Some were in work clothes; some were dressed for school; some were ready for the office. There was even a tall African American woman in full tribal regalia.

The system for choosing the jury panel was structured and gentle. The judge and each lawyer had a say in the choices, as did the prospective jury members themselves. Once the jury was chosen, they were sworn in by the judge. He gave them an inspirational pep talk about how our country is a great one because we have the jury system, which is all about helping people to settle their differences peacefully.

I listened inside myself throughout that morning and here is what I learned: our judicial system may not be perfect but it is definitely fair. I am grateful to be an American. I am grateful to live in a country where we have a system in place to settle arguments peaceably. I am profoundly grateful to know that if I am ever in a situation where I think someone else has wronged me, there is a place I can go in order to be seen and heard fairly.

The jury that day decided in my favor and of course that made me (and especially my insurance company!) very happy. But the best part about that whole experience was seeing our American judicial system in action. I even felt moved to make a patriotic SoulCollage® card for my deck.

I've been called for jury duty several times over the years but have never had to serve. In the past, whenever I've gotten that summons in the mail, I've had a knee jerk "Oh no!" reaction and a definite resistance to the whole thing. Here's something else I learned at traffic court: the next time I get summoned to jury duty, I'm going to be looking forward to it. It is indeed, as Antonio Villaraigosa, the 41st mayor of Los Angeles, once said, a privilege and an honor.

Time for Reflection

Do you have a card in your deck that expresses pride in your country, wherever you live? If not, explore your feelings about your country. What would a card like that look like?

The dictionary describes *patriotic* as: *having or expressing devotion to and vigorous support for one's country.* If you already have a card like this in your deck, spend some time journaling with it this week. What is its story? What gifts does it have for you? What does your country need from you?

SoulCollage® Resources:

Please visit kaleidosoul.com/inner-journeys-growth
The password for this page is grow
The topic to scroll down to is:
Patriotism

To learn more about EFT Tapping, please visit thetappingsolution.com

CHAPTER 36

Into the Woods

WHEN I WAS 14, my brother Joe took me to see a University theatre production of *Man of La Mancha*. That was my first experience with live "grown-up" theatre and I was totally hooked after that. I went to as many shows as I could; I memorized and sang many a show tune in the shower (and everywhere else). When I landed a job in the box office at a large regional music theatre in 1995, I thought I'd landed in heaven because one of the "perks" was free tickets to any musical, as many times as I wanted.

You can probably tell by the title of this column that my favorite musical is *Into the Woods*. The first time I saw it was when a video recording of the live original Broadway cast landed in my hands. Guess who loaned it to me? That's right, Joe! He's ten years older and one of the things we've had in common over the years is our love of theatre.

I remember the first time I watched that video. Act One brings together several famous fairy tale characters and sends each of them into the woods on a quest for their deepest wishes. There's a baker and his wife who are longing for a child. Cinderella wishes to go to the ball. Little Red Riding Hood wants to visit her granny. Jack (from Beanstalk fame) has been sent to sell his beloved cow so their family will have food to eat. Along the way they meet some other fairy tale characters: a big bad wolf, "the witch next door," and a couple of handsome princes.

At the end of Act One, everyone has received their wish. But. That is not the end of this story. I actually thought that the show was over when the curtain dropped on Act One. I even got up, put down my knitting and moved to turn off the television! But then . . . the curtain opened on Act Two and I was able to see what happens *after* "happily ever after."

Besides being a brilliantly written piece of theatre with lyrics that send us into equal amounts of laughter and tears, *Into the Woods* contains many archetypal themes about love and loss, parenting, community, birth, death, and everything in between. Since that first video viewing, I have seen the show countless times in community theatres as well on larger stages and even the big screen recently. Every time I experience it, I learn something new about myself, about life. Every time I see *Into the Woods*, I am led deeper into some part of my own story.

For this reason, I recently felt led to create a SoulCollage® card. For me, it is archetypal because each character's story has a deeper, broader meaning. When I journaled with this card, the beings on it spoke to me as one:

> *We are the ones who are on a journey. Together and separately we are seeking different things. Our journey is fraught with mishaps and wrong turns but also blessed with good fortune.*
>
> *Our gift to you is the gift of Journey with a capital J. We give you desire for a magical quest of your own. What is it that you most want? Know that you can have it and it is a journey worth taking.*
>
> *We want you to remember that you do not journey alone. Someone is always with you guiding you on your journey. We want you to know that once you get into the deep dark woods of your journey, you might feel lost but you can and will always find your way out. You can and will receive what you are questing for.*

Time for Reflection

Take a few hours out of your busy schedule this week and watch *Into the Woods*, either the original Broadway cast version or the movie that came out in 2015 featuring Meryl Streep. Try to watch it without doing anything else, and pay close attention to any theme or lyrics that touch your heart.

Make a SoulCollage® card to represent a theme that resonates with your soul and with your own life's journey. Journal with it and see what this Neter has to tell you.

If the *Into the Woods* story doesn't appeal to you, choose another movie with multiple layers of meaning that you are drawn to instead.

SoulCollage® Resource:

Please visit kaleidosoul.com/inner-journeys-growth
The password for this page is grow

The topic to scroll down to is:
Into the Woods

CHAPTER 37

The Opposite of Normal

WHEN I WAS a teenager, my life was a never-ending quest for *normal*. I wanted to fit in, wear what the popular kids were wearing, do what they were doing, listen to the same kind of music....etc. And I always felt *abnormal* because I didn't fit in. I didn't like smoking pot and drinking; I liked writing stories and playing my guitar. I didn't like Led Zeppelin; I liked John Denver. And I didn't look great in tight mini-skirts; I looked and felt more like myself in long flowing skirts and scarves.

Now I can see the wisdom of Whoopi Goldberg who once defined *normal* as just a setting on a washing machine. There really is no such thing as "normal." It's a concept thought up by the media, to get us to buy what "everyone else" is wearing, driving, reading, watching, and listening to. Even now that my adolescence is a good 40+ years behind me, I still have to be careful not to get caught up in our culture's obsessive quest for the conventional. I have discovered that trying to be like everyone else is simply a waste of my own time and energy.

Because I'm not like everyone else. And neither are you!

We are each unique, wonderful human beings with individual gifts to give the world. When we start trying to fit our distinctive, irreplaceable selves into the cookie cutter molds that society tells us is "normal," we throw away our precious chance to become exactly who we were meant to be. SoulCollage® is a priceless gift that enables us to live our unique lives and honor our particular gifts and shadows with compassion and joy.

Let us listen within to our own inner callings, and let us be true to them in spite of what is happening all around us.

Time for Reflection

Look through a few magazines and newspapers, making note of any references to "normal." Journal about what you discover.

How do the media try to influence you to be someone you're not?

Make a list of 15 unique qualities in yourself that you value. Hang the list on the wall where you can see it every day.

Make a SoulCollage® card about "normal" and/or about "unique." Allow your new card to speak to you!

Community Suit

Overview

The Community Suit of a SoulCollage® deck is important because it brings in the aspect of connection. As human beings we all crave connection; this suit gives us a place to visually honor those people, pets, and sacred places that have touched our lives. It also offers a space to pay tribute to our loved ones who have died, as well as to celebrate artists, religious figures, teachers, celebrities, authors, and politicians whose work in the world has influenced us in some way.

Whenever I draw one of my Community cards in a reading, I am deeply touched by the power of connection. Cherished pets who have left me still have things to say to me. Someone from my childhood can still inform me with wisdom today. An actor whose creative work in the world has moved me deeply can speak to me even though I will never meet him in a physical sense.

The bright lesson of our Community cards is that we are *all* connected.

CHAPTER 38

New Beginnings

MY YOUNGEST STEPDAUGHTER Merri gave birth to our first granddaughter, Victoria Grace, the week before Christmas in 2006. We went to visit the new little family in the hospital the day after the birth. Merri's boyfriend Michael was lying down with Victoria on his chest while Merri was seeing her doctor. When we walked in, he immediately stood up and asked if I wanted to hold her for a while. *Did I want to hold her?* Do stars shine in the sky at night? *Heck, yes!*

I held Victoria throughout our visit. Conversation drifted around me. I could hear the voices of Merri, Michael, and my husband, but they might as well have been speaking Greek because after a few minutes of silent sleep, Victoria opened her deep blue eyes and looked into mine.

That's it; she just looked into my eyes. There were no earth-shattering revelations. I didn't hear angels singing (well, almost!) or receive messages from Beyond. None of that was necessary because I was holding the revelation in my arms.

It seemed, as I held her and we looked into each other's eyes while everything else faded away, that other things faded away as well: outdated grudges I'd held against Jeff's ex-wife, my sorrow surrounding my own childlessness, and a multitude of past mistakes that I'd been clutching onto out of habit.

Is it any wonder that when I woke up the next morning, I was humming the words to the song *When A Child is Born*?

Time for Reflection

If there's a baby in your family or circle of friends, make some time this week to hold him or her for at least a few minutes. While you are holding the baby, meditate on the theme of *new beginnings*.

If there's no baby nearby for you to hold, look at some of your old baby pictures for a while and do the same thing. Is there some way to incorporate one of these baby pictures into a SoulCollage® card for your deck?

What can a baby teach *you* about new beginnings for your own life?

CHAPTER 39

Sacred Spaces, Sacred Places

I AM WRITING this essay from one of my favorite places in the world, Kripalu Center for Yoga & Health in the Berkshire Mountains of western Massachusetts. I've given myself the gift of a three-day stay here this week, and I am basking in the glow of the snowy mountains, healthy food, nourishing yoga classes, and most of all... the fact that when I'm here, I fall in love with myself all over again.

There is just something about this place and the energy that lives here that reminds me of who I am. As soon as I walk through the front doors, I am able to breathe more deeply. With the outbreath of stress and "doing-ness," I am better able to remember that divine spark within me.

Seena Frost, the Founder of SoulCollage®, has taught us that we can include cards for special places like this in our Community suit, which is all about connections. I really love having a Kripalu card in my SoulCollage® deck. It serves as a blessed reminder of the gifts this place continues to give me. One day last summer when I was debating over whether or not to attend a particular retreat here, I actually drew my Kripalu card in one of my daily readings! I never know when it's going to show up, but it always has wisdom to impart when it does.

Kripalu has been an integral part of my life for over 20 years. There was a period of 10 years when I didn't come here at all because I told myself that I didn't have the time. I can see now that that wasn't it at all. I was in the midst of a tumultuous period in my life, and I was buying into my Inner Critic's story about how I wasn't worth anything *this good* for myself.

After I was here last year, I set an intention to return more often. Now I realize that I *am* worth this. I *am* worth anything that gives me this much pleasure, anything that reminds me on all levels of who I really am.

Time for Reflection

Close your eyes and spend several minutes scanning back over your life. What are the places and spaces that bring the sacred spark of divinity back to your heart? Make a list. You might want to browse through some old photo albums as you make your list.

Create a SoulCollage® card for one of these sacred places. Let it speak to you of its meaning in your life.

Choose one of your sacred places and begin to make arrangements to return there in person. You are worth it. You really, really are!

SoulCollage® Resource:

Please visit kaleidosoul.com/inner-journeys-community
The password for this page is love

The topic to scroll down to is:
Kripalu

CHAPTER 40

True Community

In 2006 I was blessed to celebrate my 50th birthday, and I shared that celebration with 40 friends and family members at a festive party at our home. It was a wonderful day, one that I will remember forever, because it was a definitive moment in my life. It was the day that I finally realized what true community really is.

There were people at my birthday party from all the different compartments of my life. My oldest brother and his wife, my college roommate and her husband, SoulCollage® friends, theatre friends, breast cancer survivor friends, Jeff's brother and his partner, a family I made friends with at a church I attended years ago, and some couples that Jeff and I are friends with.

At first it was really odd to me, seeing all of these people in my house at the same time. Odd, but not so odd, because the couples were in the dining room, and family members were in the kitchen, and my SoulCollage® Sisters were in the family room. There wasn't a whole lot of mingling going on, at least not right away.

Then my brother-in-law brought out my birthday cake, complete with purple and turquoise colored sprinkles, rainbow candles, and bright, sizzling sparklers shooting out from the sides! Everyone gathered together in the dining room to sing *Happy Birthday* to me while I blew out the candles.

As they *all* were singing to me, I was keenly aware of that breathtaking moment. All of my Community was gathered around me singing, beaming at me with love and smiles that offered stiff competition to those lit sparklers on my cake.

This is the moment that I will take with me from my 50th birthday celebration. I will take it with me and treasure it forever with joy and gratitude. What better gift could I receive on this special occasion than the gift of the presence of family and friends (and the occasional cat wandering through, looking for handouts) all in one place at one time?

Time for Reflection

Throw yourself a party where all the different people in your community come together in one place.

If you can't do that anytime soon, place all of your Community cards in a big circle on the floor and then sit or stand in the middle of the circle, and spend some time absorbing all of that wonderful loving energy.

You can do the same thing with photographs if you haven't made a lot of SoulCollage® Community cards yet.

CHAPTER 41

Me and Renee Z.

EVERYONE USUALLY CHUCKLES when I share my Renee Zellweger card. I usually show it when I am leading a workshop and talking about the Community suit. They think it's amusing that I have created this card to honor a celebrity. Most SoulCollage® newbies are surprised to see that this celebrated actress holds such a special place in my deck, right alongside my parents, brothers, special teachers, and friends.

Maybe you think so too! I don't mind.

My card honoring Renee Z. was one of the first I created for my deck. I have no idea why, but I have always felt drawn to her as an actress and as a human being. Perhaps we knew each other in another lifetime; perhaps it has more to do with the "nettedness" that Seena talks about in her book.

I did spend a good deal of time fretting over my decision to make a card for this actress. Then I happened to watch her being interviewed on *Inside the Actor's Studio* with James Lipton. He asked her what other profession she might like to attempt if she couldn't be an actor and she immediately responded, "I'd like to be a writer." Something settled inside me then. I felt our connection more deeply in some unique way after hearing her say that.

I decided right then and there that it didn't matter *how* we are connected, or *why*. I could simply accept it as one of the great mysteries of my life, make the card, and enjoy it. So that is what I did! Now, when her card comes up in readings, she speaks to me of integrity, creativity, hard work, privacy, and deep friendship.

I'm happy that I created this card for my Renee. As I shared earlier, I also have one for Robert Redford, and his card speaks to me of creativity, story, power, balance, integrity, and nature. These cards are valuable to me because they help me to embrace the great mystery of the fact that we truly are *all* connected, sometimes in ways that we cannot see or define.

Time for Reflection

Look through the cards in your Community suit. Do you have a card that represents a public figure who has touched your life in some way? If so, do some journaling with it. What does this person have to say to you today? What gifts does he/she bring to you? If you don't have any Community cards yet, find a photograph of a public figure and journal with it instead.

If you don't have a card like this, make a short list of performers, comedians, musicians, politicians, or other public figures whose work or life resonates with you in some way. Then choose one, seek out images, and create a card to honor their place in your life.

SoulCollage® Resource:

Please visit kaleidosoul.com/inner-journeys-community
The password for this page is love

The topic to scroll down to is:
Renee

CHAPTER 42

Warming Our Souls

DURING MY TIME at St. Peter's Episcopal Church in Salem, Massachusetts, we were blessed to have with us a young rector named Randy, who remains to this day my favorite and "best" spiritual teacher. One of the brightest memories I have of Randy involves an older, mentally-challenged man named Ralph who appeared at our Sunday services regularly for a short while. After the morning service was over, Randy would always stand in the back of the church, shaking hands with parishioners as they left.

Ralph never got in the line of people moving towards Randy. No. He walked right up to Randy as soon as he got to the back of the church, and he stood as close to Randy as he could possibly get.

I observed this behavior curiously, without judgment, several times before it finally dawned on me what Ralph was doing. In his childlike simplicity, he was able to recognize the Spirit that was present and vitally alive within Randy's being. Ralph's natural inclination was to get as close to Spirit as he could get. It seemed to me that Ralph was simply warming his own soul by getting as close to Randy's inner warmth as he could.

Looking back on this now, I smile. I used to love being in Randy's presence as well. There was something so open and accepting and non-judgmental about him. My own soul had had immense periods of winter before coming to this church; it too was seeking warmth, and warmth it had found.

I think back on that scene often: Ralph in his shabby clothes and bright smile, tucking in close to Randy, shadowing him, soaking up the warmth of his spirit like a flower soaks up the sun. It reminds me to pay attention to who *I* am staying close to. For there are those whose presence warms and nourishes me, and there are those whose company only distracts and subtracts from me. It is up to me to sense and know the difference. It is up to me to take action based on this.

Time for Reflection

During the coming weeks, pay attention to people whose presence feeds, nurtures, and warms your soul.

Also pay attention when the opposite occurs.

Set an intention to "stay close" to those who warm your spirit. Take an action step towards this intention. Call a friend. Seek out a new community. Spend some time with someone whose place in your life you've been neglecting.

Make a SoulCollage® card for someone whose presence has warmed your own soul.

CHAPTER 43

We Are All Connected

PEOPLE TRAVEL IN and out of our lives; this is a fact. A beloved teacher moves to another state. The mother we love slowly disappears into Alzheimer's. A friend says good-bye. Our lifelong partner deserts us. A cherished pet dies.

How do we let go? The same way everyone else lets go. Painfully, with tears and heartache. Perhaps kicking and screaming. Making a SoulCollage® Community card for someone we love but who is no longer with us is one of the best ways I know to not only honor that person, but to soothe our own wounded hearts.

I learned this firsthand several years ago when I discovered that Doug, an Episcopal priest I was close to in the late 80's, had died suddenly from a brain aneurysm. He was only 53. We had lost touch over the years, so I was truly shocked to hear that he had died. In light of this, I allowed myself to grieve and that grieving was deep and raw. As I was grieving, and as I was making a SoulCollage® card to honor Doug, I realized that even though our paths had gone in different directions, we truly were *still* connected.

A few weeks after making the card, when I was journaling with it from Doug's "voice," I truly felt that he was right there with me in the room. I didn't have a vision, and it wasn't anything like seeing a ghost. Instead, I felt a deep, visceral, real connection to Doug, a connection that transcended time and space. It was incredibly vivid and emotional, and it left me with the deepest feeling of peace.

If you are grieving the loss of someone you love, don't ever doubt that they are still with you. Our community connections transcend separation, even death. It's as simple and as beautiful as that.

Time for Reflection

Create a Community card for someone you love who has died. This could be for someone you lost recently, or someone who left you a long time ago.

When you're finished, don't just add the card to your deck and forget about it. Spend at least fifteen minutes allowing that person's voice to "speak" to you using the basic SoulCollage® journal questions:

Who are you?

What do you have to give me?

What do you want from me?

Is there anything else you have to say to me today?

SoulCollage® Example:

Please visit kaleidosoul.com/inner-journeys-community

The password for this page is love

The topic to scroll down to is:

Doug

SoulCollage® Resource:

Listen to Roberta Rook's online recorded course,

SoulCollage® and Grief: A Primer for Grievers

SoulCollage.com/online-classes-recorded-primer-for-grievers

CHAPTER 44

Surprised by Love

MANY YEARS AGO I boarded a plane as part of my consulting job with an educational software company. After several years of travel, plane rides had become lonely and routine, but then I met Michelle, a chubby toddler who was sitting across the aisle from me with her mother. She had light brown curls and wide, intelligent hazel eyes. Curious and adorable, she answered my simple questions and asked her own with amazing clarity and vocabulary for one so young.

When the plane landed I waved good-bye to her and went on my way. Inside the busy terminal, I planted myself in front of the board of monitors looking for my connecting flight information. Business as usual. Another airport. Another airplane to board. Always going somewhere.

Then all of a sudden, from several feet behind me, I heard Michelle's thin, young voice again. This time she was hollering, "There's that lady! I want to give her a hug!"

I quickly turned around and there she was: little Michelle, arms flung wide, rushing towards me like a tiny divine whirling dervish. I can't remember another time when I was so surprised by love, so astonished at the exuberant, free-flowing, unexpected rush of it. As she clasped her arms around my waist, I was very aware of being held by a Love and a Grace that was bigger than the two of us.

It may have looked to passers-by like *I* was hugging *her*, but I know differently. That child was holding *me*!

Time for Reflection

Let yourself be Surprised by Love this week. Be aware of strangers as you go about your business. Make eye contact with a few of them. Notice how you are connected, even though you know nothing about them.

Be open to the possibility of surprising someone else with love this week. Give a smile to a stranger, send a card to a friend who's low, or surprise someone you love with a hug or a few moments of uninterrupted time.

Take a look at the Community suit of your SoulCollage® deck. Is there someone you love or have loved, who is missing? Create a card for them this month to honor them in your deck.

CHAPTER 45

Grounded and Rooted Together

Our lives are like islands in the sea, or like trees in the forest,
which co-mingle their roots in the darkness underground.

~ WILLIAM JAMES

WHAT WOULD OUR lives be like if we really acted from the wisdom in this
quotation? I believe our lives would be richer for this co-mingling of our
roots. I believe we would be more open to love and to the friendship that
is shimmering all around us, day to day, moment to moment.

So often we go through our days with blinders on, believing that
we are alone, that we have to carry our burdens by ourselves, that
there is no one nearby who would give a darn about taking our hand
and walking with us for a while. But if we are indeed like those trees
in the forest, then there really are many people walking the same
path as we are, many who are grounded and rooted from the same
Source.

Let us lean on one another. Let us share our burdens in the darkness and thus be strengthened to grow further into the light.

Time for Reflection

Try journaling with these questions either in words or through color and image:

- Whose roots are intertwined with yours?
- How can you help strengthen another soul today?
- What could you do to allow your own soul to be strengthened by another today?

Make a SoulCollage® card for the part of you whose roots are co-mingled with others in the ground of your being.

CHAPTER 46

Indra's Net

IT IS NO coincidence that All Saints Day and All Souls Day fall in mid-autumn when everything outside is in the full grasp of death and decay. There is a soft silence that surrounds nature as leaves let go from their stable branches and flowers drop their petals. Lush greenery turns to bright autumn colors and then to murky brown. It is natural, at this time of year, to bring to mind those who have departed this earth, those beings we have cherished who have died and left us behind.

As I remember my own loved ones who have passed on, I am reminded of the story of Indra's Net, which is based on an old tale from ancient India. In this story, there is a brilliant holographic jewel at the intersection of each strand on a mammoth, universal net. Each gem reflects each of the other jewels, and so on into infinity. Because of the interweaving of the strands of this Net, each precious stone is connected to each of the others via the intricate network of Spirit.

Our families, our friends and our pets are all unique parts of the "nettedness" that make the many one. And so are those whom we have never met, but to whom we feel irrevocably connected. These include those who have taught and reached us across the years and miles: authors, artists, musicians, actors, comedians, politicians, and religious figures. Each one is represented on Indra's net with an irreplaceable, multifaceted jewel and thus is linked to us as well.

So it is with those who are no longer with us on the physical plane. My parents, my grandparents, three beloved felines, friends, and other relations are sorely missed by my body, mind, and spirit. To know that we are still connected, even though I can no longer see them with my physical eyes, is a blessing, a helpful consolation.

When my father died 20 years ago, I was part of an Episcopal church where the rector, Randy, was also my spiritual director. The day after my dad's funeral, I vividly remember my anguish as I sat with Randy and cried. "Where is he?" I beseeched, over and over. "I saw them put his body into the ground, but where *is* he?"

I will never forget Randy's compassionate answer. "Your father is not here with you, but in many ways he is closer to you now than he was when he was alive."

To be perfectly honest, I didn't find that answer very comforting at the time, only confusing! But I felt inside of me the vivid truth of it, and I held onto it until I could better comprehend the meaning.

Today, this story of Indra's Net allows me to understand Randy's answer a little better. My father *is* still connected to me. Death does not break the connections of Indra's Net. And he is even closer to me than when he was alive because there is less in the way between us.

Time for Reflection

Make a list of people in your life who love you.

Make a list of teachers and people you've never met, but who have influenced you greatly.

Read your lists carefully. Set an intention to make one Community SoulCollage® card per month until all of these beings are represented in your deck.

CHAPTER 47

I See You

I RECENTLY SAW the movie *Avatar*. One of the many things that captured my spirit and imagination was the way the creatures of Pandora greeted one another. Upon crossing paths with another being, they would pause, touch their heart, and say "I see you." They weren't speaking of a superficial "seeing." They actually paused and looked into each other's eyes as they said it. "I see you." They were acknowledging the presence and the soul of the other.

I've been thinking what a different world it would be if we each paused just a few seconds before greeting one another. It would only take a moment to really see each other, to notice the underlying beat of Spirit that connects us all as One.

I actually tried this one day at the bookstore where I was working. During the course of a day there, I would cross paths with many people, and I was amazed at how this practice calmed my own body and made me smile on the inside. Of course, I didn't say "I see you" out loud to anyone, but I did say it on the inside, and it made a huge difference in how I served them, and in how open my heart was that day.

This is also a beautiful thing to do with the people in your inner circle, people whom you see and welcome into your heart on a daily basis. Instead of just hurrying by with a quick kiss on the cheek, how about pausing for a moment and acknowledging their presence? You don't have to say "I see you" out loud. Simply take a moment to remember who this person is to you, to recognize that spark of their soul that speaks to your soul.

Time for Reflection

How would your own world change if you practiced an internal "I see you" for just one day, with strangers and loved ones alike?

Go to your SoulCollage® deck and gather all of your Community cards.

Hold each one in front of you for a few seconds and offer that being an *I see you* from your heart.

CHAPTER 48

The Facebook Cathedral

I HAD SOMEWHAT of a religious experience on Facebook last month. If you're not on Facebook, please don't turn the page. Trust me and read on.

I had posted a link to an interesting place in Japan which lets solo diners eat with stuffed animals. I'd re-posted it from Josh Groban's Tweet because it was quite funny and completely unique. Actually, I'd had a "religious experience" on Twitter the week before when I'd tweeted Josh Groban (international recording star) a question and he actually tweeted me an answer! But I digress.

The fact is that I'm connected to quite a lot of people on Facebook. I have collected many connections throughout my life. There are people from my high school and college years, and from when I taught in Virginia. There are people from the various jobs I've held over the course of my life, activities I've participated in, as well as round-the-world SoulCollagers and Kindred Spirits.

Sometimes people comment on the things I post on my Facebook page. Sometimes they just click the "Like" button, but I always get a warm feeling inside whenever I notice that someone has responded to what I've posted. For me, it's visual proof that we really are all connected, no matter where our journeys take us.

Now, back to my post about the Japanese Restaurant. The next time I checked my Facebook page, I was stunned. Not only had lots of people clicked "like," but two of my Facebook friends were having a fun conversation back and forth! I was surprised because they were two people who had never met one another, two people I thought had nothing in common.

Lorraine, a senior citizen, lives in British Columbia and was one of our very first Kindred Spirits back in 2006. I've never met her. Pete, a quirky guy in his late twenties, was the head cashier who trained me when I worked at Barnes & Noble in 2008. *They were two people who were only connected to each other by their connection to me.* And there they were, on my Facebook page, having a little conversation about this restaurant (that I only heard about because I was connected to Josh Groban)! It literally gave me goose bumps when I saw that they were "conversing" in response to my post.

We use the story of Indra's Net often in SoulCollage® to express the reality of how all people are connected. So it's not far-fetched at all to say that Spirit touches me through Facebook every day. Every being in the world is lit by the same light of Divine Spirit. All of us are jewels reflecting the light of the One. And in each of us, all others are reflected as well. This net of connectedness goes on and on. There is no beginning, no end. We truly are, each and every light-filled one of us, connected to each and every other.

For me, Facebook symbolizes this huge sense of connectedness. Of course, we can use it as a tool that enhances our connectedness, or we can abuse it and use it for something else. It's up to us. It's always up to us.

Time for Reflection

Ponder the story of Indra's Net this week. How does it feel to know that you are connected to everyone by this nettedness?

If you're on Facebook, scroll through the list of people you're connected to there. Send a blessing to each one in your heart.

If you're not on Facebook, spend some time making a list of people you've known throughout your life's journey. Send a blessing to each one in your heart.

Make a SoulCollage® card for someone in your community whose light reflects your own.

CHAPTER 49

Celebrity Connections

I WAS CHATTING once with Seena Frost, the Founder of SoulCollage®. We were talking about a famous woman author, someone who Seena greatly admired but had not met. This woman was going to be speaking near Seena's home in California. A mutual friend had offered to arrange for them to meet. I had imagined that Seena would delightedly jump at this fortuitous opportunity. I asked Seena if she was going to go to hear the author speak and then meet her afterwards, since she'd admired her for so long.

When she told me no, I expressed surprise. Seena said that she felt she didn't need to *meet* this woman in order to feel like she was truly connected to her. She also said something that I've been pondering ever since. I'm not quoting her directly here, just trying to capture the essence of her meaning and how it came across to me: when you're really drawn to someone or attracted to someone of "celebrity" status, it's because you've both been grabbed by the same archetypal energies.

Earlier in this book you've encountered essays about my feeling connected to Robert Redford and Renee Zellweger. If you follow me on Facebook or Twitter, you've probably heard me rhapsodizing about Josh Groban. I do have cards in my deck for Robert and Renee, as well as John Denver, and several authors who are of "celebrity status." I recently made a card honoring Josh Groban's place in my life as well.

Now let me state for the record here that there are many celebrities whom I admire greatly and who have touched me deeply with their performances, words, and music: Colin Firth, Helen Hunt, Mandy Patinkin, Alan Alda, Adam Lambert, Greg Kinnear, Johnny Depp,

Laura Linney . . . . I could go on! But for some reason, I don't feel drawn to including any of them in my SoulCollage® deck.

As for Robert, Renee, Josh, and John . . . I am drawn to them in a much deeper way. I used to feel a little embarrassed, even silly, about how connected I felt to these particular celebrities, until I heard Seena express her idea about being grabbed by similar archetypes. That really resonated with me and now I celebrate these connections instead of feeling silly about them. I continue to muse on which particular archetypes have grabbed us, and I know that time will reveal all to me if I am patient.

Time for Reflection

Make a list of actors, actresses, musicians, or performers whom you greatly admire. Flip through your stacks of DVDs and CDs if you need prompting.

Look at your list and note if you feel more deeply connected to any of these public figures, in a way that goes beyond "What a great actor!" or "I love her music!"

If there are a few celebrities to whom you feel more deeply drawn, ponder what archetypal energies might have grabbed the both of you.

Do you have cards for these people? If not, go ahead and make some! Allow their wisdom to light your way, via your SoulCollage® Deck.

CHAPTER 50

Falling in Love with a Sacred Place

Wisdom sits in places.

~APACHE PROVERB

ONCE UPON A real time there was a woman named Anne Marie. She went to Alaska and fell in love.

Thus begins a real life fairy tale! But I didn't fall in love with a person. My dear husband Jeff was with me; I don't need any more of that kind of love. I fell in love with the sacred place that is Alaska. I wasn't expecting to; it was quite a lovely surprise.

I remember when I fell in love with Jeff. It too was an unexpected surprise. When I met him, I felt an instant recognition, an immediate connection, and I knew that our love would be a lasting one.

It was the same way when I first caught sight of the fjord in Alaska known as Tracy Arm. After about half an hour of slowly cruising up this fjord (on the Celebrity ship Solstice), I found that I couldn't look away. I stood in the freezing cold air of our little balcony on the ship, and my heart beat a little faster. I was thoroughly entranced. All that wilderness. No people, only trees and animals for hundreds of miles. We were surrounded by water and ice, mountains and green glacier water, the sound of eagles in the distance, the rippling of the water beneath us.

Here are some things I wrote in my journal that morning, July 21m 2014, a day that I will always remember:

Silence. Wide silence.
Silvery green water like jade.
How precious these moments are.
John Denver's spirit is still alive here.
My heart is full.
Ancient melody of silence surrounds us.
Around every turn another new vista.
This place speaks to me of Always. Forever. The beginning.
Wildlife. Wild. Life.
How does my life appear in relation to this pure unspoiled magnificence?
Every slight turn of the ship's path alters the view. It is good to alter our view and often.

Time for Reflection

Think about all of the places you have been. Are any of them sacred to you? It's hard to explain how you'll know; it's just a feeling inside, and you can trust it.

Make a card for this sacred place and give it a place of honor in your deck. Do the basic journaling with it. Let it tell you its story and its wisdom for you today. Let this place tell you its secrets.

Be aware, wherever you journey, of your inner response to a new place, a new location, a new building. Notice if you're falling in love with it! Even if it's not labeled as a "sacred space," it doesn't matter. If it's sacred to you, that's all you need to know. Let yourself fall in love.

CHAPTER 51

Heroines in Your Community Suit

I HAD NOT really thought about including heroines in my Community Suit until another SoulCollager emailed me to suggest it. She told me that she personally celebrated a different female heroine every month because she was tired of how (in America) we get days off for important men in history but not women. I was struck by the ring of truth in these words, and believe that it's a topic worth diving into.

If you don't have any cards in your deck for real-life Heroines, perhaps it's time to consider adding some!

Dictionary.com defines the word "heroine" as *a woman of distinguished courage or ability, admired for her brave deeds and noble qualities.* This definition, of course, is wide open to your own interpretation. I used to think that to be a heroine you'd have to save someone's life, or do something outstandingly brave in the face of physical danger, but now I am thinking differently.

You might know a woman in your life, or you might have read about her or seen her in a news story on TV or in a movie. This woman might have faced a difficult diagnosis with humor and a remarkable spirit. She might have given up a successful medical career to live a life feeding the hungry in Africa. Her life's calling might be to nurse abused animals back to health.

Heroines in your SoulCollage® Deck might include well-known historical figures: women who took a stand, women who changed the course of history, women who stepped into a field (politics, medicine, law, the arts, etc.) where they made a difference.

I encourage you to start thinking about and collecting images for women who are your own personal heroines, so that you can create cards for them and add them to the rich Community layers of your own SoulCollage® Deck.

Here are just a few names of women who might qualify for this category:

Clara Barton * Mother Teresa * Amelia Earhart * Susan B. Anthony * Rosa Parks * Eleanor Roosevelt * Helen Keller * Beatrix Potter * Anne Frank * Hillary Clinton * Abigail Adams * Maya Angelou * Ellen DeGeneres * Dorothy Day * Elizabeth Cady Stanton * Christa McAuliffe * Georgia O'Keefe * Sandra Day O'Connor * Harriet Tubman * Margaret Mead * Gloria Steinem * Juliette Low * Rachel Carson

Which ones do *you* personally resonate with?

Time for Reflection

Go ahead and add some of your own heroines to this list. Think about women on your journey who have inspired you to greater creativity, wholeness, authenticity, and success, however you define success. These can be women still living or already passed on. When these women show up in your readings, they will have much wisdom, strength, and hope to add to your life.

Make a card for a real life or fictional heroine who has inspired you in some way.

Don't forget to do the basic journaling questions with this new Neter. Embrace her story and notice the meaning that *her* story has for *you*.

SoulCollage® Resource:

Please visit this page for additional real life and fictional heroines to add to your list:

http://list25.com/25-bravest-leading-ladies-and-real-life-heroines

CHAPTER 52

The Teacher Did Appear

I WAS 31 years old, shopping in a crowded little New Age bookstore. Throughout my life, I'd often found solace in bookstores and that day in particular, I truly needed an extraordinary kind of comfort. I was in the throes of an overly dramatic, very difficult relationship with an alcoholic. I loved Dan with all my heart, but he was drowning in his addiction and couldn't see it.

On that day, in that bookstore lightly scented with sandalwood incense, I found a cassette tape titled simply *Peace*. There was a scene of a beautiful sunset on the cover and the marketing lingo promised "guided imagery and soothing music for relaxation, healing and inner harmony." It sounded exactly like what I needed right then, so I picked it up and added it to my growing pile of self-help and spiritually-oriented resources.

Over the next few years, I listened to that cassette tape over and over and *over* again. There were several short guided meditations which were spoken in a gentle, soothing male voice with a comforting New York accent. Restful music by Steven Halpern gently swirled in the background. I don't have the cassette any longer, and it is out of print, so I don't remember the exact titles of the meditations, but I do remember the feelings of security and empowerment that they evoked in me. Somewhere along the way, I had lost touch with the core essence of Anne Marie, and those meditations, those words, gave that essence back to me. I marveled at how I had found that tape exactly when I needed it the most.

At the age of 33, I was finally able to let go of Dan for good. Yes, I had the support of a church community as well as a couple of regular 12 Step groups. But looking back, I can see that it was the messages on that cassette that led me to *seeking* community and support because I was finally able to grasp the fact that I was worthy of, and in dire need of, a life that was free of emotional abuse and so much drama.

Flash forward to me at the age of 48. I was attempting to recover from the after-effects of my first journey with cancer. I was also attempting to integrate the difficult past 10 years of my stepfamily story. The guided meditation tape called *Peace* was long forgotten. In fact, cassettes themselves were long forgotten! But I was still seeking solace in bookstores, and at some point that year, I stumbled across a book called *A Deep Breath of Life*, by someone I'd never heard of named Alan Cohen. The subtitle was *Daily Inspiration for Heart-Centered Living*, and that really spoke to me as something I desperately wanted and needed.

A Deep Breath of Life is a book of short daily readings. Each page began with a quotation followed by a short essay by Alan Cohen, and ended with a one line prayer and a short affirmation. To say that this book breathed new life into me and opened my heart to a world of possibilities is minimizing the effect that it had on me. It didn't happen right away, and I was hardly even aware of what was happening inside of me, but that book accompanied me throughout that whole year and beyond. It reshaped me; it gave my heart a wideness that I didn't know existed.

After a year or so, I began to notice a difference inside of me as a direct result of reading this book daily. "Hmmm . . ." I thought. "I wonder who this Alan Cohen person is." So I went online and discovered he'd written many other books. I purchased several and dug right in!

Now, it wasn't simply the fact that this man had a lot of wisdom to impart. He truly did and does. For me, I resonated most with the way that he shared his wisdom, which was mainly through the mode of storytelling. He used real stories from his own experiences as well as ancient stories from wise ones past. I was filled with gratitude that I had found a teacher who spoke so directly to my heart and to what I needed at that point in my life.

At some point after delving into more of his writing, I went to his website and discovered that many of his books are published by Hay

House and that he has his own online radio show. I was excited by this opportunity to listen to him "live" instead of just reading his books, so I went online and settled in to listen.

It took several minutes before I realized that his voice sounded familiar. "Now, where on earth have I heard this guy speak before?" I wondered. It didn't hit me right away. I think it took a couple more hours of listening to that strong male voice with the comforting accent before I remembered. That cassette tape. So many years ago when I was lonely and hurting and afraid. Those guided meditations that I listened to when I so sorely needed to come back home to myself, to remember who I was, to let go of a relationship that no longer served me. *That cassette tape was also from Alan Cohen.*

How marvelous that I was drawn to this particular teacher not just once, but *twice* in my life when I was in desperate need of guidance and inner nourishment. Ever since that moment when I realized the powerful effect this one teacher had on me, I was able to viscerally understand the meaning of this golden nugget of wisdom: *When the student is ready, the teacher appears.*

Indeed. How marvelous that Spirit watches out for each of us so closely, so genuinely, so tenderly.

I recently created a SoulCollage® card to honor some of the many teachers who have graced my life over the years. Alan Cohen is the first one on the top stair!

Time for Reflection

Think back over your own life. Make a list of "teachers" who have appeared when you were ready.

Honor one of these teachers with a card, or honor all of them with a card. Let their wisdom continue to inspire you within your deck!

What particular kind of wisdom or teaching are *you* ready for right now? Sense that readiness inside of you. Offer up a prayer to Spirit that you will be led to the right teacher. Remember that a "teacher" can take many forms: a novel, a film, a song, an online course, a quotation, or something that you hear a stranger say in passing. Teachers are not only found in self-help books but in the world around us. Your teacher might be a little child, an ornery relative, a character in a novel, or even a being on a SoulCollage® card.

SoulCollage® Example:

Please visit kaleidosoul.com/inner-journeys-community
The password for this page is love

The topic to scroll down to is:
Teachers

Companions Suit

Overview

This suit of the SoulCollage® Deck represents the energetic dimension of our lives. Specifically, we create cards for this suit that give image to **animal energies** as well as our body's **physical energies**, known as chakras.

Discovering one's Animal Companions is a highly individual process and no one can tell you exactly how to do it. People use a variety of different modalities. These include but are not limited to: guided imagery, dream work, music, Shamanic inner journeys, and energy work. Paying attention and noticing what animals are choosing to claim you are also good ways to discover your Animal guides!

When Seena was creating the SoulCollage® process, she was reading a powerful little book called *Personal Totem Pole*, by Stephen Gallegos. In this book, Gallegos describes how he came to understand that a specific animal energy resided in each of his body's chakra centers. Seena adapted his teachings into what is now known as the SoulCollage® Companions suit.

The Sanskrit word *chakra* literally means wheel, so I like to visualize my chakra centers as lightly vibrating wheels of energy. My first steps into the chakras found me chatting with a Little Brown Bird in my heart chakra area. After that, I spent a little time in each of the chakras as I discovered the Animal Companions who lived in each one. It took me well over a year for them all to make themselves known to me, so don't be discouraged if you don't "get" which ones are yours right away.

Patience and self-compassion are excellent companions on this particular inner journey.

Later on my own SoulCollage® walk, I dove a little deeper into the chakras by focusing an entire month on each one. The chakra essays in this section are from that seven month period where I lived, breathed, ate, slept, and created with the seven chakras!

If the word "Companions" doesn't resonate with you, you might choose to call this part of your SoulCollage® deck any of these names instead: Animal Guides, Animal Totems, Animal Tribe, or any other label that you prefer.

CHAPTER 53

Spider Woman

YOU'VE JUST READ the title of this essay and you're probably raising your eyebrows. I assure you, it's not what you're thinking. I haven't suddenly sprouted eight legs and the ability to spin my way through thin air, rescuing lost orphans and pulling good citizens from burning buildings.

What *has* happened is that I've been sighting spiders for the last several months. The first few times I saw a spider, it was in our bathtub. "I've never seen a spider there," I thought to myself as I went on my way, forgetting about it almost immediately. But it was not long forgotten, because that spider stayed there for a few *months*. And the more I saw it, the more I wondered.

As a passionate SoulCollager, I now know something about paying attention to messages from the Animal world - if we pay attention, the Animals have messages and gifts for us.

So I began paying attention. The more aware I became, the more I started seeing spiders everywhere. I mean, *everywhere*! The kitchen sink. A living room window. The ceiling in our laundry room. Several locations on our front porch. Almost every spider I saw was in some stage of spinning a web. One had even caught a juicy little fly for breakfast! Last week I observed a tiny one on the other side of my car window while I was driving down the highway.

At first it seemed like just a strange coincidence. Then I started thinking I should look up Spider as an animal totem and see if there was a message for me. But I kept putting it off. I've never really liked spiders, and frankly, it was taking all my energy not to kill them like I used to!

A few days ago, I looked up some information on Spider to see what messages She has for us. I used a few of Ted Andrew's books as well as some online sites. In reading about this marvelous little creature, I was surprised to find that my initial repulsion had disappeared.

Now I'm off to journal about what Spider really means to me in my life right now, and to see if I can weave my own life into the web that was destined for me!

Time for Reflection

Learning about our Animal Companions is all about awareness; it's about paying attention. Make a note of any animals that you've been seeing lately. Perhaps one of them is one of *your* Animal Companions or Guides. Perhaps it simply has a message to share with you. Make a promise to yourself to be open to whatever gifts the Animals want to give you, even if the Animal who comes to you at first is not one that you particularly like.

CHAPTER 54

My Summer of Skunks

SOON AFTER WE first moved into our home in Beverly, I was continually seeing skunks in our yard, even in broad daylight, which is highly unusual skunk behavior. A few times I actually glimpsed a white skunk with a black stripe, which is another rather unusual sight.

I wasn't practicing SoulCollage® at that time, but it did pique my curiosity.

Years later, I learned that skunks offer us energy related to self-respect, self-esteem, and inner protection through intuition. As I took in that particular bit of knowledge, I realized that they had been appearing to me at a season of my life when I felt completely powerless and unprotected regarding some difficult stepfamily situations that directly affected my self-respect and self-esteem.

Coincidence? I think not!

I haven't seen a single skunk brazenly walk across my front yard since that particular summer. I believe that Skunk had a message for me that year, and I believe that if I need him again, he will be there.

Time for Reflection

Take some time this month to pay attention to any animals (welcome or unwelcome) that are crossing *your* path as you go about your daily business. Look up in the air too. And in the water. Don't discount any insect, reptile, or mammal, large or small, that piques your curiosity. Maybe it is one of your Companion Animals. Or maybe it simply has a message for you in your life right now, as Skunk had for me that one difficult summer.

Take the time. Pay attention. What is this animal saying to you today? How can he or she help you with whatever is happening in your life right now?

CHAPTER 55

First Chakra: Grounded for Life

FOR THE PAST four weeks I have focused my morning meditations on my first chakra energy center where my Animal Companion, Brown Bear, resides. Our first chakra is located at the base of the spine and is also called the root chakra.

There are so many lessons that are centered in this first Chakra energy center. The message that I most needed to hear this month was that of *grounding*. I've spent most of my life "up in my head," so this message was fairly new to me. The very thought of visualizing roots growing down from my "trunk" and into the ground had a profoundly healing effect on my entire life.

One weekend during my "First Chakra Month," I attended the wedding of my youngest stepdaughter Merri. It was a lovely occasion, but it was also fraught with anxiety for me because of my stressful past relationship with Merri's mother. The details are unimportant, but suffice it to say that Brown Bear came with me to the wedding, along with a sure sense of grounding that I'd never before experienced.

Time for Reflection

Spend some time this week focusing on your own root chakra, located at the base of your spine. Close your eyes and imagine roots growing down through your legs and anchoring you to the earth. Write about this experience in your journal.

If you have already discovered your Animal Companion for this chakra, create a card for him or her. If you already have a card, spend some time journaling with it this week. What wisdom does it have for you and your life's journey right now?

Find a way to be good to your lower body. Get a massage or acupuncture. Massage your own feet and legs! Walk barefoot on the earth and feel your connection to Nature.

SoulCollage® Example:

Please visit kaleidosoul.com/inner-journeys-animals
The password for this page is energy

The topic to scroll down to is:
Root Chakra

CHAPTER 56

Second Chakra: Going with the Flow

THIS PAST MONTH I have focused my morning meditations on my second chakra energy center where my Animal Companion, Leopard, resides. The second chakra is located above the pubic bone, below the navel, and is also called the sacral chakra.

Leopard was one of the last of my Companions to make himself known to me. I closed my eyes one night before sleep and just asked for whichever animal lived in my sacral chakra to appear. Suddenly, there was a baby leopard in my mind's eye. Well, I wasn't expecting that! But I accepted him and I gladly sought out images and made him a card.

During this month, I was fortunate to assist Seena Frost at a SoulCollage® Facilitator Training. I was present as she led us in her guided meditation with one of our Animal Companions. During this experience, I imagined myself climbing onto Leopard's back; I was able to ride with him for a long way. Facing him in conversation, I admired his sleekness, his power, his grace, his swiftness.

When Seena suggested that we ask our animal what gift it had for us, my beautiful Leopard said, "You have the same power and beauty, grace and sleek swiftness in you." I literally gasped when I heard this in my imagination, for I knew it as the truth even though my "logical" mind has been telling me I'm too heavy to be so sleek and powerful. However, in the guided visualization, I experienced the Leopard's physical characteristics as my own, and am now working with Leopard specifically on my own journey towards getting back to my natural weight.

In my readings on the second chakra, I was drawn to meditate on this area of my body in terms of emotions and pleasure. There are many other points of focus for this chakra, but right now I seem to be in a place where physical pleasure and the flow of my feelings are key points for me. Throughout this month, Leopard was with me constantly, even on days when I was traveling and too exhausted to even think of meditating.

Time for Reflection

Spend some time this week focusing on your own sacral chakra. Close your eyes and imagine water flowing through this area, easily and effortlessly. Write about this experience in your journal.

If you have already discovered your Animal Companion for this chakra, create a card for him or her. If you already have a card, spend some time journaling with it this week. What wisdom does it have for you and your life's journey right now?

Find a way to be good to your second chakra. Sway your hips to a wild musical beat. Take a warm bath. Give yourself sensual pleasure. Do something creative.

SoulCollage® Example:

Please visit kaleidosoul.com/inner-journeys-animals
The password for this page is energy

The topic to scroll down to is:
Sacral Chakra

CHAPTER 57

Third Chakra: Balance of Power

YELLOW WAS THE predominant color on my home altar this month as I focused in on the energies of my third chakra, located between breastbone and belly button. Butterfly is the Animal Companion who currently resides in this energy center in my own body. I found myself breathing deeply and more often into my solar plexus, an area sore neglected in my own life.

In my reading on this chakra, one word appeared again and again: power. Many other ideas and concepts are associated with the third chakra (authority, control, will, warmth, ease, transformation), but *power* is the one that caught my attention this time around.

According to Anodea Judith, a pioneer in our current understanding of the chakra energies, true power comes from harmony and balance: light and shadow, male and female, strength and vulnerability.

In a society where the word *power* has many negative and sometimes frightening connotations, I found it quite a paradigm shift to begin thinking of power in a positive, healthy, transformative way. I looked through my deck and found some cards that feature powerful women and men, and I placed them on my altar as vivid reminders of my own balanced power.

Butterfly was the last of my chakra Companions to make herself known to me. I discovered her "by accident" when I created a card that happened to have a lot of butterflies on it. The facilitator pointed out to me that I had placed the biggest butterfly on the card right on top of the woman's stomach! I have to admit I was a bit distressed that such a tiny fragile creature was my *power* animal. I had been expecting a larger, "stronger" animal like Elephant or Wolf. However, in spending time with Butterfly, I am realizing how much power and strength there is inherent in the complex transformation that she undergoes from cocoon to flight. I can see how her power is palpably present even though she is small and seemingly fragile. This is true power at work in nature, in the world, in my body, and in my life.

Time for Reflection

Spend some time this week to focus on your solar plexus chakra, located directly beneath your lungs. Breathe deeply into this area; feel your midsection rise and fall with each breath. What is this part of your body trying to tell you right now? Write about this experience in your journal.

What personal beliefs do you hold about the concept of power? When in your life do you feel most and least powerful? Is there some way to bring more balance into your life so that you can claim a bit more of your own power this week?

If you have already discovered your Animal Companion for this chakra, create a card for him or her. If you already have a card, spend some time journaling with it this week. What wisdom does it have for you and your life's journey right now?

Find a way to be good to your third chakra. Rub this area in slow circles clockwise. Eat something healthy that tastes good. Do some sit-ups. Breathe slowly.

SoulCollage® Resource:

Please visit kaleidosoul.com/inner-journeys-animals
The password for this page is energy

The topic to scroll down to is:
Solar Plexus Chakra

CHAPTER 58

Fourth Chakra: Wide Open Heart

THE WHEEL OF energy that spins in the center of my chest speaks to me about: balance, love, compassion, relationship, breath, openness, peace, and forgiveness. This month when I focused on my heart chakra during my meditations, I visualized this part of my body (heart and chest) surrounded with a bright emerald green light. I breathed slowly into my heart each day and as I did, I felt it opening up a little bit more . . . releasing . . . letting go of an itchy tightness that's been present for a long time.

Also during this Heart Chakra Month, we received news that my husband's rare genetic eye disorder (cone-rod dystrophy) had worsened to the point where he was officially declared legally blind. Immediate and sometimes difficult changes took place as a direct result of this, and our relationship is consequently undergoing quite a few adjustments.

Because I have been focusing so intently on my heart chakra this month, I've noticed that I am much better able to be present and open to my husband as he maneuvers through this distressing diagnosis. I have been spending more time with my own Heart Chakra Companion, Little Brown Bird. As a result, I have been better able to open my heart to Jeff. Our "nest" is still strong and sturdy, and we continue to rest and fly together.

Time for Reflection

This week, focus on your heart chakra which is located in your chest region. Breathe deeply into this area; feel your chest rise and fall with each breath. Does your heart feel open? Closed? Tight? Warm? Cool? Write about your relationship with your heart in your journal.

If you have already discovered your Animal Companion for this chakra, create a card for him or her. If you already have a card, spend some time journaling with it this week. What wisdom does it have for you and your life's journey right now?

In your daily life, notice who receives your love fully and joyfully. Spend more time with that person if you can!

Notice if your heart has closed itself off to someone in your life. This could be a good thing if you need to protect yourself. But it could be a hurtful thing if your heart is operating from past truths. See if you can tell the difference.

Find a way to be good to your heart chakra. Breathe consciously every day. Feel the air coming into and out of your lungs. Hold your hand over your heart several times a day and murmur kindnesses to yourself. Spend time with people and animals you love and who return your love freely.

SoulCollage® Example:

Please visit kaleidosoul.com/inner-journeys-animals
The password for this page is energy

The topic to scroll down to is:
Heart Chakra

CHAPTER 59

Fifth Chakra: Lion's Roar

THIS CHAKRA IS also known as the throat chakra and it is associated with creativity, self-expression, sound, communication, connection, harmony, and vibration. It is represented by the color blue. My fifth chakra Animal Companion is Lion. I don't remember exactly how Lion came to me; it feels like he has been with me forever.

As I focused on this energy center in my body, I marveled at the fact that it is Lion who accompanies me here rather than any other animal. My own life has been governed by a couple of major archetypes, one of which is Creativity. So who better to reside in my throat chakra with its exponential lessons to learn about self-expression? Lion is the King of the Jungle, strong and powerful, as is my creative life, if I allow it to be so.

Our annual KaleidoSoul Retreat happened during my Fifth Chakra Month. During our Saturday night community activity, another facilitator was leading us on a drumming journey with our animals. She asked us to make animal sounds as we were drumming. At one point, the woman to my left let out the most magnificent lion's roar I'd ever heard, and I felt the presence of Lion immediately. Since then, I've been practicing my own roar and getting pretty good at it, I must say!

It doesn't matter what Animal greets you in your throat chakra. The important thing is to listen and pay attention to what it has to teach you about your own modes of creativity and self-expression.

Also, it's no coincidence that I was working with throat chakra energy that month as some communication issues came up with my husband and I was much better able to speak up in order to begin the process of resolution. I realized that it is up to me to control the flow of energy in my throat so that it's not too open or too shut down.

Time for Reflection

This week, focus your attention and energy on your throat chakra. How does it feel? If you needed to roar, could you? Does your throat feel blocked or open? Loose or tight? Write about your relationship with your throat in your journal.

How can you express yourself more completely this week?

If you have already discovered your Animal Companion for this chakra, create a card for him or her. If you already have a card, spend some time journaling with it this week. What wisdom does it have for you and your life's journey right now?

Find a way to be good to your throat chakra. Drink lots of water. Sing along to your favorite song! Tell someone you love them. Speak out loud a boundary that you need to set. Wrap your throat lovingly in a turquoise scarf. Sip a cup of hot tea with lemon or honey.

SoulCollage® Example:

Please visit kaleidosoul.com/inner-journeys-animals
The password for this page is energy

The topic to scroll down to is:
Throat Chakra

CHAPTER 60

Sixth Chakra: Trusting My Intuition

THIS CHAKRA IS also known as the third eye, and focuses on the energy in your body that is between your eyes, in the center of your forehead. This chakra is about inner and outer vision, memory, imagination, and intuition. It is represented by the deep blue color of indigo. This is one of the first chakras that I actually understood, as intuition has played a big part in my life over the years.

On my life journey, I have learned to trust my inner promptings in a big way. For example, there was the time I placed a singles ad in our local newspaper. Of course, this was in 1991 before the advent of online dating. My intention was to improve my social life, and placing the ad felt like the best way to do that.

Notice that I said it *felt* like the right thing to do, as opposed to I *thought* it was the right thing to do. Actually, if I had relied on my rational thinking self, I never would have placed the ad at all. I had never done anything remotely like that, so it was a surprise when I felt myself inwardly nudged to do this. I had no intention of meeting a husband, but that is exactly what happened. I now jokingly refer to Jeff as "Bachelor #7."

My sixth chakra Companion Animal is Dolphin, who made herself known to me in the winter of 2004 as my 81-year-old-mother was dying. I just happened to be reading the Madeleine L'Engle novel *A Ring of Endless Light* and was totally captured by the intuitive nature of the dolphin. Also, there were many messages for me in that book about communicating in ways beyond words, which was just what I needed to be hearing as my mother lay in a coma from a series of strokes.

Throughout my life I have also (usually but not always) trusted my intuition to safely guide me through a myriad of relationships, family issues, and career changes. To me it looks like this: simply knowing on a deep level when it's time to leave a certain job, feeling at home with a particular person, being internally aware of the right time to talk about a certain issue, sensing inside of me that a particular workplace "feels right."

I intuitively "knew" that SoulCollage® was perfect for me the first time I read a description of it online. Through the years, I've discovered that the practice itself has sharpened my intuitive skills in a visceral way. Because the more I turn off my thinking brain when I'm looking for images or making a card, the more space my intuition has to operate. The more that I trust my intuition to choose the best images for me, to place them "this" way instead of "that" way on my card, the more I find myself trusting my intuition on a day-to-day basis instead of just for the "big things" in life.

Time for Reflection

Sit in silence for several minutes and focus your attention on the space between your eyes. How intuitive are you? Is there a way to give yourself more quiet time this week so that you can give this part of you time and space to grow?

Pay attention to your intuition the next time you're looking for images for your SoulCollage® cards. Consciously turn down the volume of your thinking self, and spend some time cozying up to the part of you who simply "knows."

If you have already discovered your Animal Companion for this chakra, create a card for him or her. If you already have a card, spend some time journaling with it this week. What wisdom does it have for you and your life's journey right now?

Find a way to be good to your sixth chakra. Anoint that part of your forehead with oil. Give yourself time each day to sit in silence. Use your imagination to take yourself to a beautiful place in nature.

SoulCollage® Example:

Please visit kaleidosoul.com/inner-journeys-animals
The password for this page is energy

The topic to scroll down to is:
Third Eye Chakra

CHAPTER 61

Seventh Chakra: Whispers of Love

THE SEVENTH CHAKRA refers to the area directly over the crown of one's head. This chakra is about consciousness, intelligence, divinity, and our connection to all other beings. It is represented by the color of violet. It is also referred to as the crown chakra.

One of my yoga teachers ends every class with a guided meditation. She always begins by inviting us to imagine a beam of pure white light entering our bodies at the top of our heads, and following the light, breathing it in, as it travels down through each chakra of our bodies. Whenever I experience this meditation, I like to imagine Spirit breathing that light into me from above. It is a centering, lovely practice to follow; I treasure those times of divine connection.

The other day something happened at the pet store that reminded me of this spiritual bond. I entered the store and headed for the cat food section but paused at the large rabbit cage for a moment to admire the four beautiful bunnies that were busily going about their lives. A pure brown one was snoozing in the little plastic hut. Two gray and white rabbits were nibbling on lettuce and carrots, and the fourth (pure white) was just looking around at his mates and the scenery.

I went to get the cat food and on my way back to the front of the store, a patron entered with two dogs on leashes. The dogs began barking up a storm; they were really making a racket!

As I passed the rabbit enclosure this time, the scene was completely different. All four of the rabbits were on dog-terror alert. They were sitting up, eyes wide and bright, and their entire bodies were quivering, including their silvery thin whiskers. I felt sorry for them so I stopped and spoke softly over the cage. "It's all right, little bunnies," I said calmly. "You're safe in there. Those dogs can't get you. Don't worry; I won't let anything happen to you."

Of course, they didn't pay me any attention at all. As long as they were convinced that the dogs were a danger to them, they couldn't be open to my reminders of safety and protection.

I wondered how often I act like those rabbits. On how many occasions do I freeze in my tracks, even though in reality I am truly safe? How much of my life do I spend completely terrorized, even though in reality, the Divine One is standing directly over my head and whispering love right into my very body and soul?

Time for Reflection

Sit in silence for several minutes and focus your attention on the space directly over your head. Create a conscious intention this month to connect on a daily basis with the Divine (however you choose to experience the Divine).

Ask for guidance in discovering an animal guide who will help you in opening your seventh chakra a little bit at a time so that you can walk through your life in Divine presence more often.

If you have already discovered your Animal Companion for this chakra, create a card for him or her. If you already have a card, spend some time journaling with it this week. What wisdom does it have for you and your life's journey right now?

Find a way to be good to your seventh chakra. Sit in meditation. Say a prayer. Inwardly pronounce blessings on everyone who crosses your path today. Affirm to yourself that you are beloved, that you are not alone.

SoulCollage® Example:

Please visit kaleidosoul.com/inner-journeys-animals
The password for this page is energy

The topic to scroll down to is:
Crown Chakra

CHAPTER 62

Evolution of a Heart

ONE OF THE interesting things about working with the animal energies and the chakra energies is that sometimes the animal energies change.

The very first Animal Companion I discovered was Little Brown Bird. In 2005, I was listening to Seena Frost's guided meditation on finding an animal companion. Little Brown Bird was in my heart chakra area, sitting on a nest of eggs. That's it. Very simple. I didn't understand much about all of the chakras when I began SoulCollage®, but I did understand the heart chakra. And it felt "just right" to me that Little Brown Bird was my heart chakra Companion at that time.

Over the years, I have felt Little Brown Bird's movement in my heart. I have chatted with her about past loves, about current loves, about self-love, about nesting, about flying.

A few years later, as often happens once we start to be aware of Animal energies, I began noticing that Crow was making an appearance in my life. I was seeing crows in our driveway, the back yard, tree tops, parking lots, and magazine images galore. Suddenly Crow was there everywhere I turned. I got stuck for a while in my left brain, trying to figure out what it meant, but then I realized that I had to let go of all that "figuring out" before the answer could unfold.

After a while, I began to have the idea that Little Brown Bird was no longer serving me in my heart energy center, and that Crow was taking her place. This is still happening inside of me, on a deep soul level, and I haven't yet completely explored all of the meanings and messages that this heart transformation means for me.

And that's okay. One of the biggest lessons I've learned on my SoulCollage® journey is that I don't "need to know." I *can't* control these inner changes. I don't have to control them. What I *can* do is go with the flow of them. Notice them. Accept and embrace them. And then sit back and watch what happens next.

Time for Reflection

If you know who your heart chakra Animal Companion is, pull that card out of your deck and place it front and center where you will see it often this week. Journal with it. Ask it what lessons about love and community it can share with you this week.

SoulCollage® Examples:

Please visit kaleidosoul.com/inner-journeys-animals
The password for this page is energy

The topic to scroll down to is:
Evolution of a Heart

Spirituality

Overview

The essays I've written that fall into this category have to do with topics such as forgiveness, letting go, prayer, and our relationship with the Divine. SoulCollage® weaves through all of these topics in ways that might surprise you. My own relationship with Spirit has deepened and matured because of my work with this ever-deepening process, and I hope that yours will too as you read these stories and do the suggested activities that follow.

CHAPTER 63

Stay Close: SoulCollage® As Prayer

In 2009 we adopted a beautiful yellow lab named Suzy. She's a feisty sweetheart who lives with exuberance and joy. When we first got her, I tried taking her for walks, but she was too energetic and I couldn't control her, so we signed up for a six-week training class at the local pet store.

The first commands we learned were "sit" and "stay." Then we worked our way up to "drop it," "leave it," and "wait." After that, we graduated to walking together. I thought the command for keeping her beside me would be "heel." But instead, our trainer used the word "close" as in "stay close beside me."

The next week as I was taking Suzy for her daily walks, I found myself saying the command many, many times. It almost became a chant. If she pulled too much, or tried to stray: *close, close, stay close, stay close*. If she got sidetracked too long by a certain tree stump: *stay close, close, stay close*.

After several days of this, the command "stay close" was so ingrained in me that I was hearing it in my sleep and in my dreams! One day, when I was telling Suzy to *stay close*, I had the distinct impression that Spirit was telling *me* to *stay close* as well.

It was right about that time that I was working on a *Soul Songs* news-letter issue with the theme of *SoulCollage® as Prayer*. I was trying to come up with a straightforward definition of prayer. After chanting the "stay close" mantra several hundred times on my Suzy Walks, it became very clear to me that prayer simply is this: a way for us to *stay close* to Spirit (or whatever name you choose to give The One that holds The Many).

When I pray, it is essentially a way to strengthen my relationship with Spirit (the name I choose to call God). If I stray too far from Spirit's path for me, prayer brings me back. If I get sidetracked by something that isn't good for me, prayer reminds me exactly Who I am connected to.

In my life's journey, my knowledge and expression of prayer has taken many forms. I have been in church prayer groups where praying out loud was the main mode of expression. I have sung my prayers and I have even danced some prayers. I have prayed silently. I have prayed while weeping and also while laughing. I have prayed with rosaries and mala beads and a prayer necklace that I created myself. I have prayed simple prayers and complex prayers. I have prayed while walking a labyrinth and I have prayed in grand cathedrals. I have led prayers in an Episcopal church and I have been led in prayer by a Buddhist teacher. I have painted prayers and written prayers with words.

Now I also see the wisdom in using SoulCollage® as a tool for prayer.

Time for Reflection

Wherever you are in your own prayer life, I encourage you to see prayer as a way to "stay close" to Spirit (however you choose to call Spirit).

Choose one SoulCollage® card randomly and write a prayer from the voice of that Neter.

Go through your deck and choose any cards that have something to do with Spirit, or with your relationship with the Divine. Allow these cards to advise you on how you can incorporate more prayer into your life this week.

SoulCollage® Example:

Please visit kaleidosoul.com/inner-journeys-spirit
The password for this page is divine

The topic to scroll down to is:
Prayer

CHAPTER 64

Dead-Heading as a Spiritual Practice

I DID NOT inherit my mother's green thumb. That's right; there is no "inner gardener" card among *my* Committee cards! In fact, when the flowering plants I'd hung on our front porch were dying, my mother-in-law had to tell me that I needed to start dead-heading them.

Dead-heading? I wasn't sure I wanted to do anything to my plants that included the word "dead," but she reassured me that pinching off the already-spent blossoms would resurrect the plant and give it even more life and vitality. So I took her advice and began the deadheading process. Lo and behold . . . the plant literally came back to life overnight!

Sometimes growing things need sun. Sometimes they need water. Sometimes they just need to be rid of whatever is blocking the flow of nourishment from the soil in which they are planted.

I think of this often as I am dead-heading the plants on our porch every summer and am reminded of the value of "dead-heading" in my own life as well. It's inspired me to clean out several drawers and closets that have been holding things that I no longer need.

Every time I do this, I feel lighter inside and out. I love getting rid of things that drain my creative and personal energy. Having too much clutter, or even a spattering of clutter, seems to block my ability to take in nourishment from Spirit as well.

I've also been doing some work with emotional clutter. As I sift through the pieces of my past (some broken, some gleaming, some muddy, some clear) I am more and more able to shed the tears and anger that should have been expressed years and years ago. It's a slow process and I find I must access my inner patient self. She is a grand ally for me as I do this dead-heading work.

Time for Reflection

Look around the place where you live. Take a brief stroll around your inner life as well. Is there some dead-heading of your own that you can take care of this month? It might be flowers that need the work, or it might just be one drawer, a closet, or an old memory that needs to be brought out into the light and swept away.

Remember to be kind and gentle (with the flower *and* with yourself) during this process.

Is there some way that SoulCollage® can help you do this inner work of dead-heading?

CHAPTER 65

Angels Moving the Furniture

RECENTLY I SPENT a few days moving the furniture around in my Quiet Room. I had been feeling creatively stymied whenever I walked in there, until I realized exactly what I needed. A little Feng Shui can be very good for the soul! My desk is now near the window, and my art tables are near the door. The bookcase and altar changed places also. I held every single book in my hands and dusted it, then sorted through them all and got rid of quite a few.

In a year or so, I will probably have the same feeling of being creatively blocked, restless, and wanting something different. When I notice I'm feeling that way, I will rearrange the furniture differently again. Even though I'll have a few new black and blue marks on my legs, I will be happy because the room will feel like new to me, and my creative energy will be able to flow once again.

This whole concept works on a larger scale as well. When I was in college, I had a friend in Divinity School who was helping me through a big transition. I was struggling, and the struggle was painful, even though the change I was going through was a good one.

My friend told me he liked to think of such transitions as "angels moving the furniture around" inside of him. That really caught my attention and it has stayed with me over the years. I still love the visual image that this brings: a couple of shimmery, stalwart, loving angels scurrying around on the inside of my life, shifting things around, and always for the good, no matter how many black and blue marks the changes leave on my soul.

Time for Reflection

Are you going through any transitions right now in your life? If so, write about it in your journal. Give this transition a name. If not, think back to the last big change you went through.

What happens when you think in terms of angels being involved in your life transitions?

Is there some area of your life right now, where the metaphorical furniture needs to be moved around or thrown out completely?

Make a SoulCollage® card for an inner part of you that resists changes in your life. Journal with it and let it tell you its story.

CHAPTER 66

Beyond Mind and Memory

A FRIEND OF mine once told me a story about how her brother-in-law disappeared for four days and no one knew where he was. Originally from North Carolina, he had traveled to Virginia Beach on business and went for a walk at midnight. Someone mugged him, and he ended up with a concussion and amnesia for two whole days. When he "came to," he was in New York City.

Talk about scary. Can you *imagine*? But here's where the story gets really interesting.

This man is Jewish and deeply religious. Prayer is a habitual part of his daily routine; religious rituals are part and parcel of the very fabric of his life. When he was in New York City, still not knowing who he was or where he was from, he *did* remember that he was Jewish. And even though he couldn't remember his name, he did remember the exact words of each and every one of his daily prayers.

My heart beat faster when my friend told me this part of the story. His relationship with the Divine went far deeper than his mind and his memory could allow. Even though he didn't know what he did for a living or who his family was, he *did know* that he was Jewish, and that God was a very real part of his life.

Eventually, the amnesia lifted, his memory returned, and he was joyfully reunited with his family. But this story remains with me today as a bright lesson of my own deep and personal connection to Spirit. When I think of what happened to my friend's brother-in-law, it reminds me of how *I* am known by *the One*- deeply, unconditionally, beyond mind and memory.

Time for Reflection

Do you have a Source card yet to represent The One? If not, seek out images to create one.

If you do have a Source card, set it out this week where you will see it every day. Whenever you walk past it, pause and make a gesture of love towards yourself and towards this representation of Spirit energy. You might hold your hand over your heart; you might make a small bow. Do whatever feels right to you.

Spend some time in solitude and stillness this week. Allow yourself to feel and to know that *your* connection with Spirit is one that can never, ever be broken.

SoulCollage® Example:

Please visit kaleidosoul.com/inner-journeys-spirit
The password for this page is divine

The topic to scroll down to is:
Source

CHAPTER 67

Lessons in Forgiveness

IN THE 80's, I was involved in a "scandalous" situation in the small Virginia town where I was teaching second grade. In the grand scheme of things, it wasn't a very big deal, but at that time in my life, things were being done and said by two of our school district's administrators that were untruthful and hurtful to me as well as another teacher. After the initial hurt wore off, I knew that I needed to forgive them and move on with my life, but I just couldn't see how.

A few years later, I was attending an Al-Anon Conference and wandered unknowingly into a workshop session on . . . you guessed it, forgiveness! We do indeed get what we need.

I learned some huge lessons in that little workshop:

1. To *forgive* doesn't necessarily mean I have to *forget* how I was wronged.
2. To *forgive* doesn't mean that I have to *condone* another's words and actions.
3. To *forgive* means that I am letting go of my attachment, my self-justification, and the past, because I finally realize there is nothing I can do to change it. It is what it is. It was what it was.

That was a lovely awakening for me and I'm happy to say that I was able to forgive those two administrators during that workshop, and it felt heart-lightening and sweet to be able to do so.

In the years since then I have been able to apply these forgiveness principles to several people in my life, including my mother who emotionally abused me when I was 12, a boss (she was the best boss I ever had) who stole money from our company and was fired, and another boss who demoted me unfairly (via email) after I'd been working with her for ten years. Each time that I get to that place inside where I can *let go of hoping for a better past* (as Lily Tomlin once said), I am able to forgive and truly let go.

Now flash forward to the present. I have been struggling for years to forgive my husband's ex-wife, Cheryl, for the way she hurt his kids (and me in the process) a long time ago. It's one of those things that I know I need to work on, but just can't seem to *do*.

Last month in another facilitator's workshop on the chakras, we were focusing on the Heart Chakra. You'll never guess what topic came up. *Forgiveness.* Am I not living proof that we get what we need?

So now, the time has come for me to forgive Cheryl. This is a big one. Bigger than the others I have had to forgive throughout my life. I know it's going to take some time, but I feel like I am ready, more ready than I have ever been.

I have been doing some inner dialoguing with Little Brown Bird and Black Crow, my Heart Chakra Companion Animals, and they have much wisdom to teach me about forgiveness, compassion, unconditional love, and empathy. I have also been asking Spirit for help, because I don't believe that I can do this on my own.

I can tell that forgiveness is beginning to happen because I can feel the difference in my body now when I talk about Cheryl, when I run into her at a family gathering, or when I bring up memories of that hurtful time. I can feel something shifting inside my body and my heart. I find that I can remember the good, sweet times along with the bad a little more often each time I "go back" there.

I will never completely *forget* how she treated me. I will never *ever* condone how she treated her children. But I see now that for years I have been yearning for a "better past." For years, I have been holding onto the wish that it all would have been different. But I don't have the power to change the past. It is what it is. It was what it was.

My mind is ready, and soon my heart will follow completely.

Time for Reflection

Is there someone *you* need to forgive? Spend some time this week journaling about that person and what he or she did to you. Get *all* of your feelings out. It's crucial to feel and express all of the anger, the sadness, the fear. It's important to be able to tell the story, to tell how it was for you. It's necessary to acknowledge these feelings to yourself, and maybe even to a friend who is a good listener.

Spend some time breathing into and from your heart. If you already know who your heart chakra Companion Animal is, close your eyes and imagine this being with you. Ask it what it knows about forgiveness. Ask it what wisdom it has for you about forgiving that particular person, about letting go of the way you were hurt.

Draw three cards randomly from your deck. Ask the same question of all three of your cards:

How can I move towards forgiving _____?
or
Who will help me understand how I can forgive _____?
Be gentle with yourself. Sometimes forgiveness takes time.

SoulCollage® Example:

Please visit kaleidosoul.com/inner-journeys-spirit
The password for this page is divine

The topic to scroll down to is:
Forgiveness

CHAPTER 68

All Shall Be Well

All shall be well and all shall be well and all manner of
thing shall be well.

~ JULIAN OF NORWICH

I FIRST STUMBLED upon this quotation many years ago while at a lovely
retreat center near the ocean in New Hampshire. I purchased a little
prayer card with these words and tucked it away for safekeeping. Julian's
words made me feel comforted and safe, even though my life was going
along pretty well at that point in time.

Then, as so often happens, I misplaced the prayer card and the powerful words slipped from my mind.

It resurfaced a few months before I was diagnosed with breast cancer
in 2001. Great timing, I thought, reading the words over and over as I
waited for my doctor to call me with the biopsy results. I copied the quotation onto many pieces of card stock and stuck them up everywhere: my
desk, the bathroom mirror, the computer monitor, the kitchen window.
I wanted to be reminded. I clung to those words like a drowning woman
clings to a life raft in the middle of a cold, stormy ocean.

My whole understanding of the words "All shall be well . . ." changed
forever the day my doctor told me that I did indeed have breast cancer.
I realized I was thinking that if I believed those words hard enough,
the doctor's news would be positive. But that wasn't the case at all. The

quote, to me, has come to mean that no matter *what* is happening, all really is well at the deepest core of me, at the place where Spirit resides.

I still use *All shall be well . . .* as a meditative mantra today.

Time for Reflection

Spend five minutes meditating one day this week. Use this Julian of Norwich quotation as a mantra. Breathe IN on the words *All shall be well and all shall be well.* Breathe OUT on the words *And all manner of thing shall be well.* Whenever you find your mind wandering (and it will wander), just be gentle with yourself and bring your mind back to the words. See if you can do it more than once a week.

How do you feel when you repeat these words over and over to yourself? What inner voices pop up to distract you from accepting the power and wisdom of these words? Try dialoguing with these other voices in your journal.

Create a SoulCollage® card that gives image to the part of you who truly believes the wisdom in this quotation. Or make a card to honor Julian of Norwich.

CHAPTER 69

The One and the Many

Another reason I like the word Neter is because the little
word net is embedded in it. A net is a paradoxical symbol
with different "energies," just as our Neters are. A net can
protect and hold us as we rest. Yet a net can also restrict us
and prevent us from being free. Nets can feel wonderful
or they can feel threatening. Your Neters are the same.

~ Seena Frost, SoulCollage® Evolving

When Seena Frost was creating the process that is now called
SoulCollage®, she described it as *The Process of the One and the Many*. Even
though her publisher talked her out of that rather long and unwieldy
title, I can still see much value and poetry to this name. SoulCollage®,
at its best and brightest, teaches us of *The One* that holds all of *The Many*
parts and pieces of our lives, of our souls.

Here in the land of SoulCollage®, we like to refer to these *Many*
parts and pieces as *Neters*.

Neter is an ancient Egyptian word that means *the One from which all
that exists arises*. We even make a card to honor this *One* in our decks. We
call it the Source card. It doesn't speak in the format of *I Am the One Who
. . .* to tell us its story, the way other Neters do. It simply *is*. Source holds
the space for all the other energies of our decks, of our lives.

But here's another really cool thing. The word **Neter**, in ancient
Egypt, also meant "the Many," specifically referring to gods and

goddesses who acted as guides, helpers, and challengers to the beings on earth. Seena has expanded the meaning of the word Neter to include *all* of the guides, helpers and challengers within *all* the suits of a deck. Thus, the cards in our decks each represent a Neter of our Soul. As Seena says, "We have many, many Neters, and they all come from the same one Source."

In the vocabulary of SoulCollage®, we can use the word *Neter* as a substitute for energy, presence, guide, ally, or challenger. I like using *Neter* instead of "card" when I talk about the energies of my deck. Instead of saying, "This card says to me . . . ," I might say, "This Neter says to me..." Because really, the "card" is just paper and glue and images. It's the *energy* of the card that is speaking with me, guiding me, and challenging me on my journey.

Time for Reflection

Try using the word Neter from time to time this week when referring to the energies of your deck. See how it feels.

Read the quote from Seena at the beginning of this essay, and imagine your deck as a Net. All of the Neters in your deck are connected to one another through this Net of Being.

Are there specific ways that your SoulCollage® deck protects and holds you?

Are there ways that specific Neters restrict your freedom?

Spend some time this week just sitting with your deck. Hold *all* of your cards in your hands or in your lap. Gather them in. Breathe with the wholeness of the deck; breathe with the wholeness of your beautiful self.

CHAPTER 70

Hazel the Faithkeeper

In the Native American tradition, one member of the
tribe assumes the role of "Faithkeeper."
This person's role is to remain at peace, centered in
spiritual vision, no matter what events befall the tribe.
Even if everyone else in the tribe slips into pain, fear, or
dissension, the Faithkeeper is the one person the tribe
can rely on as a lifeline to the Presence.

~ ALAN COHEN

AFTER READING THIS description of the Faithkeeper a few years ago,
I immediately thought of my mother's best friend Hazel. I called her
"Auntie Hazel" and although she wasn't biologically related, she was part
of our family "tribe" from as long as I can remember.

Hazel had been engaged to the love of her life in her early 20's, but
before they were wed, her fiancé was killed in a tragic car accident. She
never married anyone else and lived her days with her sister Lucille in
the house they had both been born in. Hazel started out working for an
insurance company in Hartford, where she met my mother. She then
began to feel a higher calling and eventually became a lay minister at
the Episcopal Church in our home town. This was rather unusual for a
woman in the 1960's, but Hazel had gifts for prayer and spiritual direction, and the church leaders were smart enough to put these gifts to

good use. She led prayer groups in the church and offered individual counseling and direction for the members of that congregation.

Auntie Hazel was always present at our Pacheco family gatherings. She and Lucille lived not far from us. When I was little I would frequently hear my mother on the phone with her. When she came to visit, I would find it particularly nice to sit near her; she would always place her hands on my shoulders, which I loved because she had a gentle, healing way about her.

When I was a teenager, my family moved into the large apartment on the ground floor of the house where Hazel and Lucille lived, and our lives became much more entwined. When my relationship with my mother continued to be difficult, Hazel would invite me upstairs to her study for long talks that helped me with my own faith. Looking back on that stage of my life, I can see how important her times with me were for my own spiritual growth.

She didn't just affect *me* with her faith. She was present with us when my dad began having medical issues and she was there throughout many long doctor visits and hospital stays. She was a gifted encourager and I know my mom was greatly comforted and eased by Hazel's faith and steady presence. Hazel prayed with us often and in so doing, she reminded us always that we were connected to a power greater than ourselves.

Looking back at my relationship with Auntie Hazel from full adulthood, I was always puzzled by the fact that I never considered her a "second mother." She was not the Earth Mother type, showering me with hugs or trying to feed me. She was always just "Auntie Hazel."

Now, reading the above description from Alan Cohen, I can see that she didn't embody the archetype of Mother. She was our family's Faithkeeper, a different texture of energy altogether. She reminded us that we weren't alone. She kept the Faith when we could not. She prompted us to trust in the Divine One who watched over us all.

Time for Reflection

Think back on your own life story. Was there a Faithkeeper in your younger years? Was there someone who kept the faith no matter what else was going on? Honor this person with a card for your deck.

Perhaps *you* were the Faithkeeper in your household, in your family or community. Journal about what that is like for you. Make an archetypal card for the theme of Faithkeeper. Or create a card for the inner part of you who keeps the faith.

Using the Cards

Overview

By now the flow of creativity has been working its magic and you've allowed its current to carry you forward on this amazing journey. However, the current is at ebb tide now. You've washed the glue off your hands and vacuumed up the paper scraps from your floor. Now what? There are beautiful SoulCollages strewn all over your dining room table or your bedroom floor. And you might be left with one big question... what do I *do* with them?

The essays in this section are offered in the hopes of giving you some suggestions and experiences with working with the cards individually and as a whole. *Making* the cards is an important part of the process. It's fun and it enables you to learn a bit about yourself. Going farther and actually using your cards enables you to access deeper layers of your soul. You activate your imagination and your intuition, and you develop a sacred trust in your own ability to know who you are and what your particular expression is in the world.

CHAPTER 71

The Forest or the Trees

USUALLY THE ONLY people who see my SoulCollage® cards are those who attend my workshops, along with my monthly SoulCollage® group. I look at and work with at least two of my cards almost daily, but something happened recently that made me realize that I've been looking at my *cards*, but I haven't actually looked at my *deck* in a really long time.

My sister-in-law Jan was at our house for a large family birthday party. She brought along two French foreign exchange teachers who were staying with her that week. During the course of the evening, Jan mentioned to the teachers (Anne and Michelle) that they might be interested in my work. So I happily told them about SoulCollage®. They started asking questions, so I brought out my deck and set it on the coffee table in front of us.

More questions followed, and we spent another hour and a half just talking about the process and the cards and the images on them. A few times during the conversation, Anne pointed a few things out to me that I'd never noticed before. "You have many strong, colorful, vivid women in your deck," she said in her lilting French accent.

"I do?"

She nodded vigorously and pointed to quite a few of them. I then showed her a few of my "darker" cards, and explained their shadowy side, but she insisted that *even these* dark cards were of strong, vivid women.

I also showed her two new cards I'd made the week before, both of them with the theme of aging gracefully. "Yes," she nodded. "I find it interesting that both of the backgrounds are landscapes of Africa."

"Really?" I said in total amazement, squinting more closely at them. She was right! I hadn't even noticed!

"You also have lots of minority women on your cards," she added after several more minutes of animated conversation in French with Michelle (who did not speak English as well as Anne).

By this time I was incredulous and completely fascinated. I hadn't asked for this feedback, but it was thrilling to me nonetheless. It seems that I'd been focusing on the individual cards in my deck, but not really seeing its wholeness and totality, which had something very special and important to tell me.

Time for Reflection

Spread all of your cards out on a big table, or the floor. Look at your deck as a *whole entity* this week and ask what it (your deck as a whole) has to tell you about yourself. Notice any recurring themes and symbols.

Don't forget to write your thoughts down. Remember that *you* also are a whole being, not just one of your parts.

CHAPTER 72

The Transformation of Lucius Malfoy

I LOVE IT when a SoulCollage® card tells me an important story about my life. And I love it even more when several cards together tell one story. This story of Lucius Malfoy involves a deep look at two shadowy parts of my inner world. It's a wonder-full healing story of transformation that happened inside of me with the loving guidance of my therapist, Fran.

Read my transformational story about Lucius Malfoy and Dobbie here: KaleidoSoul.com/story

The password for this page is *malfoy*.

Time for Reflection

Now, flip through the cards of your deck. Notice if any of them were created around the same time. If you look at these cards together, do they have a story to tell?

Do any of them tell different pieces of one story about your life?

Discern if any of your cards have similar characters or symbols on them. Maybe these cards have a joint story to tell you about your life.

Choose three to five cards (or more if you have the time) and put them in the order that you made them or the order that feels right for them to be telling you a story. Write the story that they have to tell.

Choose one card that shows a shadowy aspect of your inner world. Spend some time journaling with it, getting to know its story, and finding out what its gifts to you are. Then create a card that represents its brighter side. For example, in my story there is a card for the part of me who believes I am not enough, and after I worked with that for a while, I made a card for the part of me who believes that I *am* enough.

CHAPTER 73

Completely Random, Completely Divine Daily Readings with Your Deck

I'VE BEEN PRACTICING SoulCollage® since 2005, and if there's *only one* piece of advice I would give people for working with their Decks, it would be this:

Use your cards to do readings.

One kind of reading is a consistent practice that I call Daily Readings. Or Every-Other-Daily Readings, as the case may be. Go ahead and try it! Every day (or every other day) this week, draw one or two cards randomly from your Deck. Set them on your altar or desk and allow them to keep you company throughout your day. Better yet, if you have five or ten minutes, do a little journaling with each one. Just a couple of *I Am the One Who . . .* sentences and a few sentences that begin with *What I have to say to you today is this . . . .*

Here is how I did my own short reading today. I closed my eyes and took a few quiet breaths. I silenced the inner chatter and allowed myself to attune to my cards. I asked, "Who has something to say to me today?" And then I waited for inner guidance about which part of the Deck to choose from.

The card I drew is the one that honors my adult niece, Stephanie. We share the same birth month and day, as well as a passion for theatre, books, writing, and art. As soon as I turned this card over, I took a sharp breath in and felt tears starting in my eyes. Why? Because two weeks ago, she had a stroke (yes, a *stroke!*) and is currently on a long road to recovery. She has been constantly in my thoughts and prayers and dreams. And now, here, suddenly, my SoulCollage® card for her rests in my hands as well. Coincidence? I think not. I haven't drawn her card in *years* in a daily reading.

Here is the writing that I did with this card, and it only took a few minutes to do this. I say this to point out the fact that some people think that they don't have time for Daily (or Every-Other-Daily) Readings. But you do!

I Am the One Who is your niece. I Am the One Who loves you and looks up to you and who shares many of the same soul prints. I Am the One Who is creative and colorful and who loves life passionately. What I have to say to you today is this: I am deeply connected to you. I am strong and vibrant and I will be okay. I will be more than okay because of the love and community of family and friends that surrounds me. I am remembering those months when you were going through your cancer treatments and I know that if you got through all of that, then I can get through the recovery that lies ahead for me. I Am the One Who loves you so much.

See! It's really that simple. And that powerful. Doing consistent readings like this is a beautiful way to stay connected to yourself, your community, and the divine.

Now a word about the randomness of it all. It would seem like there is no rhyme or reason to the cards that you randomly draw. But there is a sweet divinity to the randomness. Why is it that I drew Stephanie's card *today* when it hasn't appeared in years? And why is it that my beloved cat Scooter's card showed up *every week* throughout the month before he died? I am so grateful for that because it made me pay more attention to him during those weeks, and after he was gone I was glad that I had spent that extra time with him.

The cards we draw when we do these readings may be random, but there is distinct divinity woven into the process as well.

Time for Reflection

Commit to drawing one or two cards every day (or every other day) this week.

Place the cards where you will see them often throughout your day.

Set aside five-ten minutes to do the very short journaling activity that I demonstrated above.

SoulCollage® Example:

Please visit kaleidosoul.com/inner-journeys-using
The password for this page is feast

The topic to scroll down to is:
Stephanie

SoulCollage® Resource:

Read Anne Marie Bennett's e-book:

Completely Random, Completely Divine: Doing SoulCollage® Readings

KaleidoSoul.com/soulcollage-e-books

CHAPTER 74

Completely Random, Completely Divine Focused Readings with Your Deck

ANOTHER KIND OF reading you can do with your deck is what I call a Focused Reading. This is when you think of a question that you want answered, pose the question to your deck, and draw three or four cards randomly to help you answer it.

Here is a focused reading that I recently did with my own deck. Last month I was thinking a lot about my older brother, John, and how out of touch we've been over the last several years since Mom died, even though we had been very close when I was younger. I had emailed him a few times to see how he was doing and had not heard back from him. I felt anxious about this lack of response, so I went to my Deck and asked: Who has insight to share with me about my relationship with John?

These are the three cards I drew randomly and here is what they said to me:

Patience - *I Am the One Who is sitting still and looking out to sea, waiting. I Am the One Who is sheltered in this cove. I Am the One Who is alone. I Am the One Who is calmly waiting for something or someone. What I have to say to you about your relationship with John is this: You have taken steps to reach out to him, dear one. You can't force what isn't happening. It's all about the tides, see? They come in and they go out. In nature as well as relationships. Trust. Be still. Focus within. Be patient.*

Mystic - *I Am the One Who is covered in a black cloak, holding a crystal ball. I Am the One Who is rising out of a multi-faceted diamond. I Am the One Who* *looks into the ball, who holds the ball reverently and steadily. I Am the One Who stands in front of Spirit, the Container of all things. I Am the One Who sees, who knows, who understands. My message to you about your relationship with your brother is this: hold steady. Do not give up. Keep looking and searching for ways to reach out to him. He is dear to you and you are dear to him. The only thing you can do is honor yourself. Because you were close when you were younger, does that mean you need to be close now? What exactly is making you sad? Look within, and see!*

Stripey Shadows - *I Am the One Who looks outside. I Am the One Who is looking towards the light. I Am the One Who is made up of light and shadow. I Am the One Who is accepting of the light and the dark parts of me. I Am the One Who knows that one cannot exist without the other. What I say to you about you and your brother is this: it is about balancing the light with the dark. You cannot have any relationship that is all golden, all the time. Open your eyes and look around you. Closeness with others comes and goes. It must be worked at, held closely, intentioned into being. Do you have that intention with your brother? Does he? Do not think that all is light or all is dark. Simply remember that all is well.*

As always, when I do readings like this, I was pleasantly surprised by the answers I received. It was exactly what I needed! Because of the wisdom and guidance I received here, I was able to realize that he and I are very different now than when we were younger, and that it's okay for us not to be as close now as we were then.

I was able to find a way to reach out to him differently, and it has made a difference in our relationship. I am now holding an intention of kindness and compassion for him, for me, and for our relationship. This new intention has replaced the anxiety tenfold.

Time for Reflection

Think for a while about what is going on in your own life right now. Make a short list of situations, challenges, or difficult relationships that you are facing.

Choose one from your list and turn it into a question.

Go to your Deck, draw three cards randomly, and do the above exercise with them.

Journal about what you received from this reading.

SoulCollage® Examples:

Please visit kaleidosoul.com/inner-journeys-using

The password for this page is feast

The topic to scroll down to is:

Three Card Reading

SoulCollage® Resource:

Please visit kaleidosoul.com/cardreadings

CHAPTER 75

Spring Cleaning My Deck

April prepares her green traffic light
and the world thinks Go.

~CHRISTOPHER MORLEY

HERE IN NEW England, we've had some warm days this past week. I can feel spring in the air; my body is waking up, beginning to stretch and unfold like the flowers that grace our front yard. My heart is looking around and saying "There *is* another season besides winter!" We've got a little ways to go before the "green" that Morley speaks of in the above quote, but my mind, heart and body are all whispering, "Go!"

When I notice that I am feeling like this, I get in the mood to create new beginnings. I pull out all the files in my desk organizers, recycle old papers, throw out craft projects that I'm no longer interested in finishing, rearrange the items on my art table, hire someone to help with the heavy yard work.

When I start to feel this urge towards organizing, paring down, rearranging and sprucing up, I feel led to consider my SoulCollage® deck also. This week I pulled out my big stack of cards, as well as my "reserve deck." Seena advises us never to throw away any of our cards, no matter what, as they are all bright and beautiful pieces of our soul. I keep my deck in my mother's old stand-up sewing basket, which has a deep basket on top for my current cards, and a shallow basket at the bottom where I keep my reserve cards.

As I approached this sacred time of Spring Cleaning, I lit a candle and closed my eyes for a moment in a silent prayer for guidance and insight. Then I dusted off the cards I'd placed in the lower basket, and looked at each one, just briefly: noticing the card, allowing any memories associated with the card to surface, and permitting my inner wisdom to tell me whether or not to add it back into my deck at this time. I was surprised to find some cards there that I hadn't thought about in a long time, cards that seemed to be relevant to me again now, so I gladly added them to my current cards.

Then I went slowly through my deck, breathing with each card, and continuing to ask for guidance to know whether it should stay or "go" for now. I was able to put a good number of cards into my reserve pile, which made room for about the same number of new cards that I've made in the last several months.

In this way, I am creating a living, breathing SoulCollage® Deck, which is in a state of flowing, perpetual change. I love the simple fact that, as I change, my Deck changes as well. It's simply a matter of being still, breathing, and paying attention.

Time for Reflection

Take time to do some "spring cleaning" with your own deck this week. Spend a quiet, holy moment with each card. Does it still have energy for you? Is it relevant to your life today? Is this a card whose wisdom has something to offer you in a card reading? If the intuitive answer to any of these questions is "no," then place the card in a special box or place. You don't have to call it your Reserve Deck. You can call it whatever you want!

Does your deck have a beautiful home? If not, it's time to create one. Discount stores often have wonderful and inexpensive beautiful boxes in many shapes and sizes. You could even purchase a lovely shawl and wrap your cards up in it. Use your intuition and imagination to give your deck a sacred space in which to reside.

SoulCollage® Example:

Please visit kaleidosoul.com/inner-journeys-using
The password for this page is feast

The topic to scroll down to is:
Sewing Basket

CHAPTER 76

Every-Other-Daily Readings

It was as clear a reading as he had ever done for himself.
Marvin wandered through the landscape that the cards
laid out for him, nodding to the images:
"Yeah, I know you. How you doing?"

~ ELIZABETH CUNNINGHAM,

THE RETURN OF the Goddess: A Divine Comedy

In the above quote, Marvin is a wanderer, traveling the world, seeking a place to settle. He has a well-loved deck of Tarot cards that he carries with him. They offer him guidance and support just as our own beloved SoulCollage® decks give us balance and encouragement.

Mariabruna Sirabella, a SoulCollage® Facilitator and Trainer worldwide, likes to say that making the cards and never working with them is like cooking a five-course gourmet dinner and never taking a bite! Think of each of your cards as part of a luscious meal that is continually being created and served by your own soul. Dive in and savor the many flavors!

One way to do this is by using your cards for Daily Readings. Or, as I like to say, Every-Other-Daily Readings. Instead of setting my expectations too high, I give myself some forgiving inner space when I tell myself I will draw a few cards from my deck every *other* day instead!

The best thing about this practice is that it isn't complicated and it only takes five or ten minutes. I love these short readings because they keep me in touch with all the bits and pieces of my inner and outer worlds, on a consistent and regular basis.

The way it works is this: every day *(or every other day!)* go to your deck, draw two cards randomly, then write for a minimum of five minutes from each card that you drew.

What exactly do you write from each card?

1. A few sentences that begin with *I am the one who . . .* to get you warmed up into that Neter's energy. If it's a card you've worked with before, these might flow easily. If it's a new card that you've never written with before, you might want to spend a little more time on the *I am the one who . . .* sentences.

2. After that, write a few sentences prefaced by:
   What I have to say to you today is this:
   or
   My message for you today is this:
   or
   Today I want you to know (or remember):

That's it, in a SoulCollage® nutshell! Now, keep in mind that you can choose one card per day to do this; you can choose two or three. It might vary depending on the amount of time that you have. Seena Frost chooses two cards every day. One of her cards is always a Community card, and the other is randomly chosen from among the other suits. You can create this practice however you choose!

Feel free to take longer than five minutes per card if you like. Sometimes the cards have much more to say and if we give them a little time, all kinds of treasures and golden light pour out of them directly onto the page and into our souls!

As you continue to practice writing with and reading from your cards, you will find that you have an ongoing relationship with each one. Doing these daily readings keeps me in constant contact with my inner voices, my circle of beloved community members, the spirit guides and archetypes who work on my behalf, as well as my chakra energies and my animal guides.

Remember the character Joey on the old sitcom *Friends?* Whenever he met a beautiful woman, he would ease on up to her and say, "How *you* doin'?" That's exactly what we're doing when we do these short, consistent readings with our own blessed Neters. I feel exactly like Martin in the above quotation whenever I turn over the beautiful cards I've chosen in these wonderfully random readings: *Hey, I know you! How YOU doin' today?*

Time for Reflection

Create and begin your own Daily or Every-Other-Daily reading practice with your cards.

Be gentle with yourself as you go. There is no "right way" to do this and no one is going to come by and check up on you! If you skip a few days, just acknowledge that, give yourself a hug, and start again.

Take your time. As you turn over a card, take a moment to breathe with it and smile at it (if you can). Say inwardly (or aloud if no one else is around!), *I know you! How you doin'?* And then give this Neter time and space to respond.

CHAPTER 77

Coming Home to Our Decks

ONE OF MY wisest teachers was an Episcopal priest named Randy. I've written about him before because the lessons I learned from him were many and deep. As a priest, Randy would often have his Bible with him. Whether he was giving a sermon, leading a Bible study, making a home visit, or speaking to the parish women's group, his Bible (standard black, worn cover, wispy thin pages, one long silken red page marker) was nearly always in his hands, almost like an extension of his body.

I remember being in awe of the ease with which he held his Bible open on his lap, gently ruffling through its pages to find a certain passage or highlighted note. It seemed to me that the Bible was a part of him, patiently awaiting his personal applications of the wisdom held within. There was such a sense of connection between Randy and his Bible: a wondrous flow, a give and take, a partnership. He seemed as at home with his Bible as his Bible seemed with him.

At the time, I was filled with a gentle longing to be able to handle my own Bible the same way, with such a calm sense of patient authority and connection. Today I notice that I seem to have transferred my longing to my SoulCollage® Deck. As I hold my cards on my lap and in my hands, I feel a deep archetypal connection to them that is similar to Randy's passionate yet subtle connection to his well-worn Bible. I *come home to myself* every time I pick up a card, hold the deck in my hands, do a reading.

Time for Reflection

Set aside half an hour this week and simply *hold* your cards in silence. Gently flip through the cards, admiring them in passing. Breathe in the beauty of your own soul.

Don't *do* anything with the cards. Don't initiate conversations with any of them. Simply *be* with them in silence, noticing each one, maybe sending sweet smiles of gratitude towards them. Use this time to settle into your deck and . . . *come home to yourself* in a new way.

CHAPTER 78

Romancing the SoulCollage

It is the relationship with the card that counts, not how
good the art is.

~ KYLEA TAYLOR

I ALWAYS TELL the people in my classes that the whole point of
SoulCollage® is not to be creating beautiful works of art, although I like
to quote Will Rogers when I say *I never met a SoulCollage® card I didn't like.*
I truly believe that every SoulCollage® card ever made, is being made
right now, or ever will be made in years to come, is beautiful, simply
because it reflects a bit of a person's soul.

Maybe now you're wondering what the point of making the cards
really is, if it's not to be creating beautiful art. Well, my friend, I will tell
you. We make SoulCollage® cards in order to *create deep relationship with
ourselves.* And in the process, we sometimes also create deeper relationships with others and with Spirit.

In the long run, we are *making meaning*, not making art. We are creating *relationships*, not just collages.

A new SoulCollager recently stood in front of my deck, reverently
running her fingers over the many cards contained in the beautiful
box. I watched her for a while. Now and then, she would pull one of my
cards out and hold it in her hands, gazing at it with a smile on her face.
Sometimes her brow would crease into a frown. After she had flipped
through both stacks of my cards, she turned to me and said, "You have

relationship with one of your cards. Try sitting down with the cards and your journal, and doing the *I Am the One Who* . . . exercise with each of them.

SoulCollage® Resource:

Please visit kaleidosoul.com/soulcollage-cards-interpreting for more information about journaling with one card at a time.

CHAPTER 79

You Get What You Need

I WANT TO tell this story as a tribute to trusting the process that is SoulCollage®, and as living proof that even though we don't always get what we *expect* when we do a SoulCollage® card reading, we do get exactly what we *need*.

My husband and I generally have a good relationship. He is very easy-going and I am a bit more "high maintenance," so sometimes we argue. In the midst of one such argument a few years ago, I stormed into my study, slammed the door, and grabbed my deck of SoulCollage® cards. I'm sure this is not the quiet, calm, meditative posture that Seena had in mind when she wrote about creating sacred space for our readings! However, it was an accurate reflection of how I was feeling in that particular place and time, so I let it be okay.

I quickly blurted my question out loud to my deck. *Who will help me figure out a way to straighten out this quarrel that Jeff and I are in right now?*

I took a deep breath, closed my eyes, and grabbed one card out of the hundred in my deck, then turned it over. I was expecting to see my Peaceful Warrior, or maybe even The One Who Pauses, or perhaps a card about listening or compassion. But . . . no. The card I had drawn was my Community card for my husband!

In spite of how angry I was, and in spite of how quickly all of this occurred, without my usual sense of reverence around doing a reading, I was immediately catapulted into stillness. Just looking at his smiling face on the card reminded me how much I loved him. And then I began to laugh. Talk about the Universe having a sense of humor . . . here was a perfect example!

Drawing *Jeff's* card in response to my question about how to resolve an argument with him was exactly what I needed to help me through that argument. It wasn't the card that I *expected* to see, nor was it the card that I *wanted*. Instead, it was exactly the card that I *needed*.

Time for Reflection

Think of a situation that is bothering you today. Maybe something is stirring up anger in the depths of your being, or perhaps a relationship is more challenging than usual.

Now, holding that situation and that anger in your mind, go to your deck and quickly, without thinking too much, draw one card.

Spend a few minutes in your journal with the wisdom of this one card. What does it say to you today? What does it say to you about your situation? Your anger? Your other feelings?

SoulCollage® Example:

Please visit kaleidosoul.com/inner-journeys-using
The password for this page is feast

The topic to scroll down to is:
Jeff

CHAPTER 80

Silence is Golden

FOR SEVERAL YEARS I have been in the habit of randomly drawing two SoulCollage® cards from my deck during my morning Quiet Time. I always do a little journaling with them as well. Whatever I choose to write, it always involves giving them a voice, letting them speak, and listening to what they have to say as I write.

I highly recommend this process of doing a daily reading with your deck. It's a beautiful way to keep in rhythm with your life, and to stay in touch with all of your Neters.

A few weeks ago I had to do without my daily dose of words. I was scheduled to work several early morning shifts at the book store, and because of this I had to miss my daily morning Quiet Times. I would look longingly at my deck before grabbing my coat and car keys each morning.

One day, in frustration, on my way out the door, I drew two cards from my deck, took a quick peek at them and just brought them with me for the day. I didn't journal with them; I just let them rest in the notebook that I kept with me when I was working. When I got home, I set them on my Altar for the rest of the day.

I was really surprised at how powerful this was!

I had always thought that if I drew a card from my deck, then I had to write from it. It had never occurred to me that a Neter doesn't have to express itself to me with words. Simply letting one or two keep me company throughout my day made a huge difference in the way I approached my life that week.

Surprisingly, I found that my Neters had a lot to "say" even though I wasn't doing any writing.

I'm not discounting journaling with the *I Am the One Who . . .* process. Not at all. I'm just suggesting that once in a while, it's okay to allow the silence to speak its own wisdom to our souls.

Time for Reflection

One day this week, try this experiment and see if it resonates with you. Draw two cards randomly from your deck, and let them hold space for you throughout the day. You might put them on your own Altar, display them on your desk, or carry them with you in your Day Planner.

Just let these two cards accompany you without picking up a pen and notebook.

What happens? Does it make a difference in how you think and act and feel throughout your day?

CHAPTER 81

The Gift of Wholeness

VERY EARLY IN my SoulCollage® journey, I had an experience with my deck that has stayed with me all this time. I still think of it whenever I browse through my cards. It makes me smile inside. For me, this is exactly what SoulCollage® is all about.

When I got married in 1995, Jeff already had three children from his first marriage. After a few years together, I decided that these three were enough for us and I gladly helped him raise the older two. However, even though my childlessness was a conscious and loving choice, I was surprised to discover that I still felt much grief and sorrow around this decision. These feelings become magnified and exaggerated every year around Mother's Day. I have struggled with this every year since I made the decision to not have children . . . until I found SoulCollage®.

By May of 2005, I had been making cards for several months and had about fifty cards in my deck already. Mother's Day morning came, and I woke up brim full of intense emotion; absolutely all of it was dark and shadowy. I recognized the feelings reluctantly: heavy sadness for the children I never had, spiny anger at my stepchildren for pushing me away in their adolescence, slimy guilt for not being a better stepmother, and some gritty self-pity muddying all of it.

On that Mother's Day in 2005, I felt certain that my day was doomed to be a miserable one. I gritted my teeth and vowed to get through it as best I could.

Then I spied my beautiful SoulCollage® deck sitting on my art table. "I know," I thought to myself. "I have cards for all these layers of darkness

I'm feeling. I will find each of them and then I'll journal with them. Maybe that will help me. That's what SoulCollage® is for, after all."

Thus began my search for the cards that represented the twisting dark emotions that were dizzily spinning in my soul. I knew they were in there: my childlessness card, the card for shame, my inner angry voice, and the one that I call "Less Than."

But then an interesting thing happened. As I was searching for all those shadowy parts that were getting in my way, I found some *other* cards: my niece Stephanie who is very precious to me, my Creativity card, inner teacher Neter, and my Angel of Sorrow who is the Being who comforts me in my sorrow.

My whole sense of self and soul shifted that day. The sorrow, anger, and guilt lifted as I was reminded that there is so much more to me than all of *that*.

I was already madly in love with the process of SoulCollage®, but after this experience, everything shifted for me. I finally "got" what SoulCollage® is all about. It's not just a tool to help us get in touch with our shadows. It's not just an artistic device to help us remember who we are. It's a divine gift that brings us wholeness.

Time for Reflection

At some point this week, give yourself 10 minutes of quiet time and sit down with your deck. Flip through your cards, one by beautiful one, and sense your own perfect wholeness. Yes, there are dark parts of yourself and your world, but there are bright parts as well.

If it feels good, divide a piece of paper in half and list the dark Neters on one side and the brighter Neters on the other side.

You might not even need to make these lists. Maybe just sitting with the wholeness of your deck will be enough.

CHAPTER 82

The Questions Are in the Cards

SOMETIMES I GO to my deck with a question about my life, and sometimes I just draw a few cards and ask, "What do you have to say to me today?" Lately, it seems like my questions are met with more questions.

For instance, one of the cards I drew in a reading this winter is one that I call The High Priest of Hiding. I warmed up by writing some *I Am the One Who . . .* statements from his voice and then asked, "What is your message for me today?" He said, *What masks are you currently wearing . . and for whom . . . and why?"*

Well, that startled me a bit. I don't remember a Neter ever answering *my* question with one of its own!

Later that month I drew my Creative Child Neter and at the end of my journaling with her, she asked, *How can you activate my energy this week?*

Another time I drew my Order from Chaos card and she closed our dialogue with a question also. *What inside of you today needs clearing? What, in your internal world, is in disorder/disarray/chaos? How can you create order from this?*

Wow! These questions were definitely right on target for me, and led me to deeper journaling adventures. They definitely gave me something to think about!

Recently, I drew my card for the regional music theatre where I used to work. Its message for me that day was: *Transformation occurred when you were part of this community. What transformation are you in now and what community are you a part of that can help you with this?*

Even more recently, I drew a Neter whom I lovingly call Our Lady of Perpetual Disappointment. She said: *I am the one with the sad face. I am the prim and proper one who says "Poor me." I am the one stuck between the craggy rocks of my expectations. I am the one who is blue, sad, and disappointed. I am the one who is always wishing things were different. My message for you today is this: What disappointments are you still carrying? How can you release these expectations that keep you stuck?*

Each time a question like this comes from one of my cards, I am surprised and delighted as well as a little vexed. How can I not answer? The reading isn't over until I've listened inside and begun to really answer the question that came forth for me.

Oh, the wisdom that my SoulCollage® cards coax out of me!

Time for Reflection

Go ahead right now and draw two cards from your Deck, randomly. No peeking!

Do some *I Am the One Who . . .* journaling from the voice of each card, just to warm up to their energy a bit.

Then ask each card any one of these questions, and see what it tells you:

- What do you have to say to me today?
- What message do you have for me right now?
- Is there something that you want me to know in my current situation?

If it replies with another question, allow that question to burrow deep within you. The questions that our cards ask us hold deep wisdom and insight, and are gifts that can lead us into amazing and unexpected answers.

SoulCollage® Examples:

Please visit kaleidosoul.com/inner-journeys-using

The password for this page is feast

The topic to scroll down to is:

Questions

CHAPTER 83

Questions and Answers

SEVERAL YEARS AGO in my work with a creativity coach, I was continually being led to ask questions - not of her, but of myself, and of my life. And not only to *ask* the questions, but to *listen within* for the answers. This is the biggest thing I learned: sometimes the answers take a long time to appear!

I have also learned that if I wait patiently, the answers will come to me. I just have to get to that quiet place inside, that tender place of waiting, and then allow myself to be there with the question. Sometimes it's easier than others, and it all depends on the question.

SoulCollage® readings with my deck have been a wondrous assistant in helping me to listen for and hear the answers. Seena Frost teaches us that the question we ask is the most important part of any reading that we do. It's important to spend quality time thinking of and wording the question so that it resonates deeply. It might even take longer to think up and word the question than to do the actual reading!

Our SoulCollage® decks are priceless tools that help us to "live with the questions." Our cards are jewels simply shimmering with hidden answers and meanings. Let us use them with reverence and intention.

Time for Reflection

Think of a question that is spinning around in your mind right now. It might be a question about your life's journey, something you're struggling with in a relationship, or just a topic that you're curious about. Be sure it is not a yes/no question or a question with a specific answer.

Here are some examples of questions you might ask:

Which Neters can help me with my relationship with _____?

Who can give me wisdom/advice about my career path?

What suggestions do you have about getting my body back to a normal weight?

Why do I have a hard time playing and being spontaneous?

There are more examples of questions in Seena Frost's book *SoulCollage® Evolving*.

Write your question on a blank piece of paper, or in your journal. Then randomly choose three cards from your SoulCollage® deck. If you don't have a deck yet, choose from a friend's deck, or go to SoulCollage. com and use the cards in the upper right corner for your "personal card reading."

Look at each card individually and ask it what it has to say in response to your question. Record its answers in your journal. Read back what you've written and see if there is an action you can take today in response.

CHAPTER 84

Three Bright Ancestors

MY OLDEST BROTHER Joe has always been the historian in our family, the "keeper of the family history." I have never been interested in family trees or who begat whom much beyond my grandparents on either side. I understand the need to know, to define, to understand one's origins. It's just that the details never really called to me or drew me in. Because of this, I've felt somewhat disconnected from my "family heritage."

And then I made a SoulCollage® card. Ah, isn't that the way all good stories begin? See the link below to take a peek at this card.

At first, my card seemed to be about the woman on the left. Whenever I drew it, she spoke to me about body image and distress over the disfigurement of my left breast from cancer.

Then a year ago, I found myself face to face with this card during a daily reading, and the stone figures on the right dominated the energy of the card in a way that I could not ignore. I couldn't get them to "talk" to me right away, so I wrote a detailed description of the card to get the imaginative juices flowing. *There is a nude woman in this card, standing behind what looks like shattered glass. On the right side of the card are three stone figures. They are not looking at the woman. They are looking beyond her. They are bathed in light of different colors - golden brown, bluish green, and yellowish green.*

After this, the words flowed more easily and this is what they said to me:

We are here to represent three of the Bright Ancestors who are watching over you at all times. We know that you feel like your body is disfigured. We know that you don't like how your body looks when you see yourself in the mirror. But we are looking beyond that. We are looking past it, over it, beyond it . . . to something bigger. We can see the Bigger Picture. We see Spirit. Spirit is the Big Picture. Spirit holds the Mirror.

We invite you today to stop looking down. To look up at your beautiful self in the Mirror, to nod affirmation of your beauty, and then to look up and Beyond as we are doing. We invite you to do this because seeing the Big Picture changes everything. Seeing the Big Picture changes how you see yourself, and how you see and respond to Life. We know that you are a loving, giving, creative, joyful being of Spirit. We know you. You are of us. You are known and loved exactly as you are. Can you take comfort in that? Can you allow this knowledge to give you courage to look at yourself in the mirror and call yourself beautiful?

As you can imagine, I was blown away by this reading. For someone who never paid much attention to my ancestors, I was suddenly feeling deeply connected to them!

Time for Reflection

Take a look through your SoulCollage® deck, or through the stacks of images you are collecting. Are there any that might be whispering to you of love and ancestry? Pay attention as you allow these images to speak to you. Remember that you *are* connected to those who have gone before you, in deep and intimate ways, even if you don't know their actual names. SoulCollage® is the perfect medium for them to reach out and touch you in this moment.

You might want to take a look through your deck and choose a card that is a "puzzlement" to you. Instead of starting with the *I Am the One Who . . .* exercise, try writing a detailed description of the card first. Take 5-10 minutes to do this, and see if it becomes easier to slip into the voice of the card afterwards.

SoulCollage® Example:

Please visit kaleidosoul.com/inner-journeys-using

The password for this page is feast

The topic to scroll down to is:

Ancestors

CHAPTER 85

So Many Possibilities . . .

So Little Time

ONCE I MADE a card simply because I loved all of the colors. When I first worked with it I was focused on the windows in the background. They seemed to be windows of possibility. I was thoroughly enchanted with this card and the possibilities that it represented to me. *Use the link below to witness this card.*

The next time I drew the card, I seemed to be obsessed with the woman lying upside down and backwards on the sloping triangle. I was mesmerized by the peaceful expression on her face as well as the core strength that kept her from sliding down the ramp. At that time in my life I needed a reminder of simple balance.

This same card appeared a few weeks ago in one of my Every-Other-Daily Readings. I had just spent a good half hour journaling about how overwhelmed I was with all of the choices that were facing me, in regards to a daily practice. To meditate or not meditate? Perhaps I should journal instead. Listen to some guided imagery? Read Mark Nepo's latest book? Take a walk? Do a SoulCollage® reading? Play in my art journal?

I found myself struggling to decide which practice to commit to and found that I simply could not choose because they were *all* good choices! I couldn't go wrong with any of them. However, having so many choices was overwhelming me to the point of inaction. This is a pattern that has appeared in my life over and over again. Can you relate?

After my journaling session, I was still a little frustrated so I did a card reading and this was one of the cards that appeared! Lo and behold, she was saying something different from the other two times I'd "talked" with her. Even better - she was saying something totally relevant to what I was experiencing right then. Listen:

I Am the One Who rests actively against a backdrop of colorful windows. I Am the One Who is perfectly poised and balanced even though I am upside down and backwards. I Am the One Who is no longer distracted or overwhelmed by all those bright windows of possibility. Instead, I trust that when the time is right, I will know which window to move towards and open.

My gift to you today is this . . . I want you to know, to remember, to practice this: close your eyes and go within. It is the best way to move through this anxious overwhelm you are experiencing. Yes, you have "so many choices" and they are ALL so colorful and appealing. But there is a time and a place for each of them, and that time and place is not All At Once! Close your eyes and go inside. Don't go to ANY window until you receive inner direction first.

It's also very interesting and serendipitous that just that week I'd been having a conversation with my good friend Cheryl F. about this very thing. It was nice to know I wasn't the only one overwhelmed with the many choices available to us for daily practice! At one point, Cheryl said something that resonated deeply. "The only consistent thing we really need to be doing every day is going within and paying attention to what we're being drawn to."

That same week, this card showed up with colorful wisdom for me in direct alignment!

This is an excellent example of how our cards can mean one thing one week and something else at another time. Always be open to the possibilities that your cards bring you!

Time for Reflection

Have you ever been overwhelmed by the many spiritual practices available to you? Journal about your choices and make note of times in your life when you've deliberately *not chosen* because it was so overwhelming.

This could also apply to other areas of your life. Have you ever walked into a clothing store and not being able to choose? How about bookstores? That's a great place of overwhelm for me sometimes. So many books... so little time!

How would your life be different if you made *listening inside and checking in with yourself* the daily practice instead?

Make a SoulCollage® card that gives image to this whole idea of closing your eyes against distractions and choosing from an *inside place* instead of an *outside place*.

SoulCollage® Example:

Please visit kaleidosoul.com/inner-journeys-using
The password for this page is feast

The topic to scroll down to is:
Possibilities

CHAPTER 86

Interesting Conversations

WHILE READING A book about Tarot recently, I came across an idea that I thought would be fun to try with my own deck.

Randomly draw one of your own SoulCollage® cards and don't peek! Then randomly draw a card from a different image-centered deck. Again, don't peek just yet.

For the example I'm sharing here, I used Joanna Powell Colbert's *Gaian Tarot Deck*, but feel free to use any other. You could also randomly select one from an app or online.

Next, turn both of the cards over and sit with their images and energies for a few minutes. Notice similarities and differences. Then begin a dialogue between these two Neters by having one of them begin with *I Am the One Who . . .* And see what happens!

In this example, I drew my own card, Comfortable in My Own Skin (CMOS). The card from the Gaian Tarot is Ace of Fire which I have renamed Baby Snake (BS) because that is the central figure on this card.

CMOS: I am the one who is sitting here in the light of the sunset, sipping my tea and enjoying my life.

BS: I am the one who is just hatching out of this shell.

CMOS: I see! You are just a baby! You are so new.

BS: And YOU are so old!

CMOS (laughing): Yes, I have been around a lot longer than you, Baby Snake.

BS: What am I doing here? What will happen next? Where will I go?

CMOS: That's only for YOU to decide. Look around you, take your time. You've been in that small dark egg for a long time. Give yourself some time to get used to the light and the air first.

BS: So...this is life, huh? Do you know anything about living that can help me?

CMOS: Yes! Life is to be enjoyed! Savored! It's important to like who you are. In other words, you're a SNAKE, so don't go trying to be a bird or a cat or anything else.

BS: Huh. That makes sense I guess.

CMOS: And since you're a snake, you'll be shedding your skin from time to time.

BS: Really? I don't know if I'll like THAT.

CMOS: Oh, you will. You'll be ready for it, when it happens. Look at me! I can't shed my actual skin because I'm not a snake, but from time to time, I shed my clothes, which is sortof like a second skin that humans wear.

BS: And you LIKE doing that?

CMOS: Oh, I do! I came into the world naked like this and that's how I'm leaving someday, so I figure I might as well enjoy and appreciate it while I can.

Time for Reflection

This exercise is a fun, creative way to get to know your cards better. Try it yourself this week, at least once. Randomly choose one card from your own deck and one card from a different visual deck. Turn them over and sit with them for a couple of minutes, getting in touch with their energies.

Then set your timer for 10 minutes and begin! Allow these two Neters to dialogue with each other. Even if you do not know the exact meaning of either card, just imagine what these two beings would say to each other.

Have fun!

SoulCollage® Example:

Please visit kaleidosoul.com/inner-journeys-using

The password for this page is feast

The topic to scroll down to is:

Conversations

Tips for Powerful Card Readings

OVER THE YEARS I've been asked many times about doing SoulCollage® readings with our decks. From my own experience, here are three tips to help you improve the accuracy and value of your readings:

1. Center yourself first. If you approach a reading while your mind is thinking of 22 unrelated things, the answers you get to your question will often not make sense. Be sure to take a few moments to relax and compose yourself before you begin to select the cards. You will be amazed at the difference this makes.

It might be as simple as closing your eyes and taking three slow in-breaths and out-breaths. You might take ten minutes of quiet meditation, or chant a prayer that centers you. When you do this, you are slowing yourself down enough to clear your mind of anything except the question at hand. You are calming your left brain and opening your right brain up to your deepest wisdom.

You might like to use this prayer shared with us by *Kindred Spirit Dot Everhart* in Pennsylvania:

> *To the Many and the One: Thank you for these cards that have come to me to share my journey. Open my mind and my heart to receive the message and the meaning you have for me as I ask a question of you, the Many and the One. Guide me to see the Many and the One in these images. I honor the Many and the One created within me and beyond me. I Am the One Who was created, is created, and will be created anew again within this circle of love. So might it be. Amen.*

2. Keep your question specific and focused. If your question is vague or unformed, your Neters will find it difficult to give you clear guidance. If you can make your question crystal clear, and hold it in your mind without being distracted by other thoughts while you are working with your cards, you will often be deeply moved by the insight reflected back to you in the reading.

For example, instead of asking, "What do I need to know about my marriage?" try asking "What wisdom do you have about the part I play in my marriage?" Instead of asking "Who has guidance regarding my career?" try inquiring, "What do I need to know about the next step for my career?" or, "Why do I feel stuck in my current job?"

3. Try not to overuse the readings. Consulting the cards many times a day, day after day, is self-defeating. As a good rule of thumb, you probably shouldn't consult the cards for the same question more than once a week or even once a month or longer. Even if you "don't like" the cards you drew or the answers you received, give the reading time and space to inhabit your soul. You may find yourself growing into the answer, and understanding may take a while to seep in.

Many years ago I did a reading where I asked my cards, "What is the next step I should take with my writing?" I don't know what I was expecting, but I certainly was not expecting my "Heavy Self" card to show up. At the time, I was so puzzled by this Neter's appearance that I confess I made up an answer just to get myself through the reading (I was in a small group at the time.)

Over the years of listening to my Inner Writer, I have often thought of how my Heavy Self appeared when I asked about my writing. Very recently I was startled to *finally* see the connection: when I am truly giving my Writer Neter full permission to simply write whatever she feels like writing (and often), my weight and eating issues simply are not forefront. This is a huge understanding for me in what feels like a lifetime of struggling with my relationship with food. I had no idea that my Writing Self was such an integral part of my healing!

I share this just to remind you (and myself!) that sometimes when we ask a question in a reading, and we turn over a card, we're distraught. We want to put it back. It makes no sense. It seems ridiculous. My best suggestion is to work with it anyway, even if its meaning and message is unclear in the moment. Allow it its special place at your table.

And know that at some point in the future, you will grow into the answer.

Time for Reflection

Give yourself the gift of a card reading with your deck this week. Consult your cards about something that's "up" for you right now in your life.

Be sure to find a way to slow your mind and calm yourself before you begin. Spend some time crafting a clear, focused, specific question instead of a general one.

Notice your inner reaction after you have asked your question and turned over each card. Are you happy to see a certain card? Distressed over another? Neutral about any? Know that it's perfectly natural, and don't put any cards back. Trust that they showed up for a reason, even if that reason isn't exactly clear at the moment.

Acknowledgements

I AM MOST grateful to Seena Frost, who created the gift of SoulCollage®. Thank you for following your deepest heart and passions in order to birth this gift to the world. I am grateful that you saw something special in me and invited me to be a SoulCollage® Trainer too!

Kylea Taylor, your encouragement, support and literary expertise mean the world to me. You have been an incredible role model for me during the last 10 years.

I thank Noelle Remington, who facilitated the very first SoulCollage® workshop I ever took and whose presence made me want to be a SoulCollage® Facilitator too. You coached me that first year as I was creating and growing KaleidoSoul, and I'll never forget how gentle you were at coaxing all of my gifts out of me.

Karen Mann, you guided me through those first awkward years as I was learning the ins and outs of the SoulCollage® process, and I will always be grateful to you for holding my hand clear across the world!

Karen Regina, thank you for lending your editorial wisdom to this manuscript. This book is much clearer and easier to read because of you! Your support across the miles is palpable to me and I thank you for your friendship as well.

I am grateful to the Reverend Randy Lord-Wilkinson whose spiritual guidance and direction flows through so many of my life lessons. I feel immeasurably blessed that our paths crossed in Salem, Massachusetts so many years ago.

Abundant thanks to each and every SoulCollager who has joined the Kindred Spirits membership over the last 10 years. You have supported our KaleidoSoul mission to continually bring bright inspiration and community to SoulCollagers around the world, regardless of their level of experience.

I am grateful to Mary Hutchinson, Kate Robinson, Jean Lendall, and Debra Zagaeski, who have served as my ever-faithful KaleidoSoul Assistants over the last decade. I could not do this work without you.

Thank you to Kimee Doherty, who dedicates herself to creating five lovely KaleidoSoul newsletters each month. I send you all the information in a Word document, and you give me back a beautiful, professionally formatted newsletter that our members around the world anticipate with pleasure. I absolutely, positively could not do any of this without you!

Marti Beddoe, I am so grateful for the tender loving purple care that you put into our friendship. Your compassionate heart inspires me every day.

Cheryl Finley, our soul friendship means the world to me. I fully appreciate our long talks about everything under the sun.

Ricia Fleming, thank you for listening to me always with an open heart. Our conversations and "show and tell" sessions always feed my soul.

Thank you to my feline triumvirate – Sasha, Scooter, and Minnie. Even though you are no longer with me, I feel your presence daily. You taught me about unconditional love and you helped me through all of the hard stuff.

Thank you to God's gorgeous creatures who grace my days now – Suzy, Louis and Seymour. You are teaching me about lightening up, trusting, and going with the flow. You continually bring me unconditional love and deep grace, and I don't know what I'd do without you.

And last but never least, I am grateful to my husband, Jeff Bennett. The unconditional love and support you have blessed me with has been a solid rock that I turn to again and again. Thank you for always acknowledging that I am a writer, and for your acute business advice as I've grown KaleidoSoul over the years. I love you with all my heart, and then some.

Resources

Want to learn more about SoulCollage®?
Visit these online sites for inspiration galore:

KaleidoSoul.com
SoulCollage.com

Become a KaleidoSoul Kindred Spirits Member and receive SoulCollage®
inspiration 24/7.
Use coupon code NEWBOOK and save $5.00 for a full year.
KaleidoSoul.com/members

Take your SoulCollage® deck with you without lugging around your
heavy cards. Use the iOS App at iTunes.

Watch a comprehensive video on the SoulCollage® process. Suzie
Wolfer, Facilitator and Trainer in Oregon, demonstrates card layouts
and working with a new card, as well as talks about the process and the
four suits:
http://newconnexion.net/watch/index.cfm/Suzie_Wolfer

Interested in becoming a SoulCollage® Facilitator?
See current Trainings listed here:
SoulCollage.com/facilitator-training

Into the Heart of SoulCollage®
87 More Thought-Provoking Essays That Explore

Committee Suit
Shadow
Council Suit
Difficult Times
SoulCollage®: The "Big Picture"
The 4 Seasons
Self-Expression
Everything I Need to Know I Learned from TV

Available January 1, 2016

Visit kaleidosoul.com/inner-journeys
for more info

Made in the USA
Lexington, KY
06 September 2016